saving 'generation next'

Achieving universal healthcare by
restoring the health of generations to come

Debi Waldeck

New York

Book I of the Series,
IN THE BEGINNING... *there was wellness*

IN THE BEGINNING...*there was wellness* ®
saving 'generation next': Achieving Universal Healthcare by
restoring the health of generations to come.
Copyright © 2008 by Debi Waldeck

Please send your comments to:
info@justdebi.com

ITB...There was Wellness
1420 NW Gilman Blvd, Suite #2323
Issaquah, WA 98027
www.justdebi.com

"saving generation next" ISBN# 9781890427511
Library of Congress Control Number: 2008941477

Cover Design and Layout by Brickhouse Studio, LLC
Edited by Jeannine Mallory, MPA
Proofread by Tyler R. Tichelaar, Ph.D. and Adrienne Bell

Printed in the United States of America
Aviva Publishing
2301 Saranac Avenue, Ste. 100
Lake Placid, NY 12946
518-523-1320
www.avivapubs.com

DEDICATION

To all of you who have wondered, "What are *those people* doing that makes them, Healthy, Well? Fit? Thin? Happy? Wealthy?" or "Why can't I find 'the magic bullet'?" or "Why doesn't it work for me?"

For all of you who suffer needlessly,
I dedicate this book to you.

No *ONE* is chosen; we are *ALL* chosen. Yet only a few heed the call. Why? Because many of us just don't believe that we can achieve greatness. You were designed for greatness. All you need is a blueprint that will lead you to physical, emotional and financial prosperity.

I am grateful to all of you
as we begin this journey.

What people are saying about
Debi Waldeck's new series,
IN THE BEGINNING... *there was wellness*

—————— ❋ ——————

Debi Waldeck's book is an incredible public health statement! Her extensive research and direct approach to human wellness can move you from crisis to excellence. Empower yourself with her knowledge.
~ Chris Bledy, Author, *Beating Ovarian Cancer*

"Debi Waldeck has made a personal journey into and through the ineffable feeling many of us have that more medication is not the answer to restoring our health. Through her years of exploration, she has developed a profound understanding of the relationship between our body's absorption and health, and, similarly, between our thought processes and wealth. If you care about becoming healthy, wealthy, and wise— and if your desire is more than idle curiosity—then the series, 'IN THE BEGINNING...*there was wellness* is truly a no-nonsense blueprint to the good life. Her approach achieves that rare balance between the comprehensive and the practical."
~ Dr. Milan Moore, Cascade Orthopedics

"WARNING! Choosing to read this book means you are ready to take responsibility for your life! Debi Waldeck's Wellness Blueprint will lead you away from society's often misguided version of reality to a much more positive reality full of health, self-love and abundance for yourself and a beautiful example for the world. 'IN THE BEGINNING... *there was wellness*' is a vital step to your own, new beginning."

~ Geof Kaufman, Author of *Mastering Your Choices*

"Debi has been a close friend for over 15 years. I have always admired her unstoppable energy. Debi thinks outside the box of traditional medicine and is passionate about helping others prevent disease and overcoming disease with wellness. Debi is an expert in training not only on the missing link between health and disease and sustaining optimal health but also successful life building strategies; she captivates the lives of many with her sense of humor and her ability to communicate.

~ Teresa Carney

"Debi has given the world a step by step plan that gives us the opportunity to live life with purpose, passion and power. I am blessed to have this opportunity to help spread the word about her good works. With this plan, prosperity and your life's aspirations are imminent."

~ Mylai Tenner, *"The Gold Boot Guy"*

"Debi has passionately addressed issues she has dealt with and many of us have had the same or similar issues. Her definition of the four L's is amazing. Longevity, Laughter, Lifestyle and Leverage just about covers it all, bless her heart. Anyone who has strife or stress in life needs to read Debi's books. Well done Debi!"

~ Jim Edmundson, Author of *Bullets I've Dodged*

"As a convention, conference and seminar speaker Debi Waldeck has helped countless numbers of people transform their lives, physically, emotionally and financially. Debi is a highly sought after speaker with a tremendous ability to present her studies in a way that everyone can understand and apply. 'IN THE BEGINNING... *there was wellness*' is a must read and reference series for every home.

~ Orv Owens, Ph.D., Author of *Relationship Selling*

Listening to Debi speak reminds me of advocates and pioneers such as those depicted in Lorenzo's oil, or Jenny McCarthy as she sought to improve the outcome of her autistic son. Debi offers the indelible spirit of a mother who in helping her children has helped all of us. Thank you Debi.

~ Helen Barker

About the Author

At the heart of Debi Waldeck's journey and subsequent discoveries, was the desire to save her son. Diagnosed with an autoimmune disease as a young adult, Debi had no idea that the subsequent medication may cause complications in her unborn child. Eight weeks into the pregnancy, Debi was told 'abort the baby'. In a moment of prayer, a word was given, "you will have a healthy baby boy and his name will be Joshua Daniel." The promise ignited Debi to search for answers, never doubting that Joshua would be whole and healthy. Her journey led to profound discoveries uncovering the root to autoimmune disease and reasons behind the nation's fourfold increase in childhood chronic illness, to include Asthma, Eczema, ADHD, and more.

The end result is, a child who was born with a significant heart defect and suffered numerous chronic health conditions during the first seven years of life, is now whole and healthy with no surgical or pharmaceutical interventions.

You need to be afraid. You are in control. Disease is not a mystery once you understand how the immune system's development coincides with the development of the infant intestinal tract.

There is a profound relationship between wellness and absorption.

It's Time to Wake up and Make a Change

When I was a young man, I wanted to change the world. I found it was difficult to change the world, so I tried to change my nation. When I found I couldn't change the nation, I began to focus on my town. I couldn't change the town and as an older man, I tried to change my family.

Now, as an old man, I realize the only thing I can change is myself and suddenly I realize that if long ago I had changed myself, I could have made an impact on my family. My family and I could have made an impact on our town. Their impact could have changed the nation and I could indeed have changed the world.

~Author: Unknown Monk 1100 A.D.

THE STORY OF DEBI'S BEE

The name Deborah is of Hebrew origin and its meaning is 'Bee'. *Debi's Dialogue* is found throughout the book series and is represented by a Bee icon. Bees create a honeycomb naturally made up of hexagonal prisms. The symmetry of the honeycomb was considered by philosophers of old to represent divine harmony in nature. Therefore, the construction of the honeycomb and the Bee itself, are known as symbols of wisdom and insight.

"Bee shows us we can accomplish what seems impossible by having dedication and working hard. It asks us to pursue our dreams with incredible focus and fertilize our aspirations. Bee teaches us to cooperate with others who have similar goals so we can learn how to help each other."

BOOK REVIEW

November 16, 2008
Tyler R. Tichelaar, Ph.D.,
Author of *The Marquette Trilogy*

saving 'generation next'
Book One in the 'IN THE BEGINNING...
there was wellness' series

Debi Waldeck
ISBN: 978-1-890427-51-1
Aviva Publishing (2008)
Debi Waldeck is an author after my own heart. Like
me, she set out to write one book, but she found
so much information she had to break it into three
volumes, and even then, each book in her new 'IN
THE BEGINNING...*there was wellness'* series is so packed
with information to help you improve your health,
finances, and overall well-being that you will want to
go back and read it again and again.

In saving 'generation next', the first book in the series,
Debi Waldeck is up front in telling us her personal
story. She is not a doctor, scientist, or health expert in
the traditional and professional sense. She is a woman
who has suffered with health problems and watched
her children suffer likewise, so she went searching
for answers. The information she found made her

question the media, doctors, and the advertisements constantly blasted at us by pharmaceutical companies. Debi decided it was time to get to the bottom of the health crisis affecting her family and millions of others, and now she is sharing her research findings with the world in this phenomenal new series.

In early adulthood, Debi was diagnosed with an autoimmune disorder. She was given medication that was not supposed to affect women or their children during pregnancy. She became pregnant soon after. While she cannot prove the medication did affect her child, doctors now recommend the medication not be given to pregnant women, unless the mother's condition is so dire, that medication is the only alternative. Ultimately, Debi's son was born with numerous health problems. During her pregnancy, the doctors told Debi she would have to abort her son because of medical complications. Instead, she listened to her inner wisdom that told her she would have a healthy child. Even when her son was born with several health issues, she did not give up but began her journey to make him and later his sister, healthy again. Through many tests and experiments she has led her family to healthy eating, and her stories will inspire the reader to do the same.

One of the most interesting personal examples Debi provided was of her son's reaction to peanut butter.

When she went to her son's school, she saw he had a dazed look and barely acknowledged she was there. She had sent him to school with hummus and pita bread, but when she asked the teacher what he had eaten for lunch, she was told some of the mothers had catered a special lunch that day, and it included peanut butter. This event happened in the days before it was discovered how many people had peanut allergies. Debi experimented by having her son write his name on a piece of paper. She then gave him a dose of peanut butter and had him write his name again—the contrast was unbelievable—the second version of her son's name was crooked, misspelled and scribbled. It was through such experiments, many more severe but just as telling, that Debi Waldeck has explored the body's reaction to specific foods.

Throughout this first book, saving 'generation next', Debi Waldeck reveals many mistakes made by modern food processing and current ideas on childbirth and child raising that have resulted in illness for millions of people. Most importantly, because the majority of children born since World War II were not breast-fed, they failed to receive natural inoculation of probiotics from their mothers. As adults, these children, and now their children and grandchildren, have likewise failed to breast-feed their babies. Consequently, many infants now have health issues at birth, even needing stomach antacids because they do not have the bacteria required so their systems can fight illness. Children's intestinal walls are immature and need the natural inoculation provided when they are breast-fed so their intestinal systems can strengthen and likewise, their immune systems develop properly. No wonder so many people today have serious and chronic health issues. Waldeck includes a great deal more information about how to reverse this situation in her goal to save 'generation next' before it is born.

Debi Waldeck consistently backs up her information with scientific findings. She has an impressive number of resources that she quotes from throughout all her books, and especially this first one. She has read numerous magazines and books and talked to experts on health, nutrition, biology, and how the body in general processes food. No one can doubt Debi Waldeck has done her homework, and she gets an A+ not only for doing the work, but the conclusions she has found. Like all good overachievers, this book was not enough. The only thing that will prevent readers from wanting to read it again immediately is the desire to see what she says in the next two volumes of this phenomenal series, one of the strongest Health and Wellness series of recent years. Two thumbs up for IN THE BEGINNING...*there was wellness*! It will change not only how you think about your body, but it will change your relationship with yourself.

CONTENTS

ACKNOWLEDGEMENTS

First and foremost, thank you to my husband and biggest fan, John, for your continued support, admiration and love. I thank my daughter who was born eight weeks premature, a C-section baby who spent her early weeks in an incubator. Her will to live is why I will never be afraid for her. Thank you to my son Joshua for being a catalyst for my work. You are why I worked so hard to compile this information. My parents have blessed me because they taught me to dare to believe we can be greater than our circumstances. I have been surrounded by much inspiration and support from my family, my sisters and brother. My mother-in-law a two time, 20 year cancer survivor, began her quest for wellness many years ago and has provided me much insight and inspiration.

Thank you to all my friends; your belief in me sustained me throughout this project. Special thanks to Nellie Bell, Deanna Aadland, Judy Stark, Linda Brickey and so many more who repeatedly brought guests to my lectures and participated in sharing the information concerning the relationship between wellness and absorption, helping countless people become well again. I was sustained through this process of completing my series each time I conducted a lecture, with all the guests you brought. My reward is and has always been the look of understanding and hope on each of their faces.

Thank you to all the teachers and writers who came before me. **Great is the written word!**

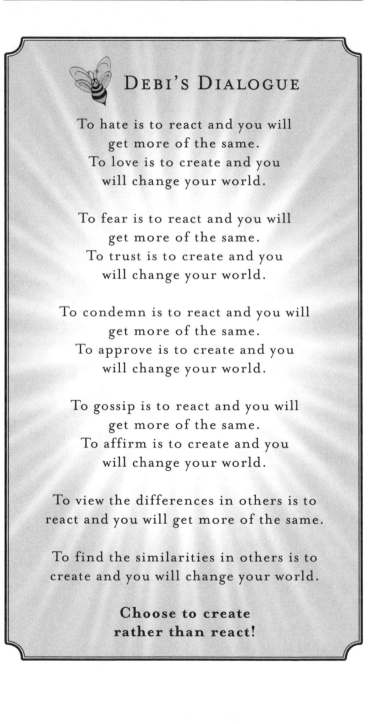

DEBI'S DIALOGUE

To hate is to react and you will
get more of the same.
To love is to create and you
will change your world.

To fear is to react and you will
get more of the same.
To trust is to create and you
will change your world.

To condemn is to react and you will
get more of the same.
To approve is to create and you
will change your world.

To gossip is to react and you will
get more of the same.
To affirm is to create and you
will change your world.

To view the differences in others is to
react and you will get more of the same.

To find the similarities in others is to
create and you will change your world.

**Choose to create
rather than react!**

IN THE BEGINNING...
there was wellness
SERIES INCLUDES:

saving 'generation next'
Achieving universal healthcare by
restoring the health of generations to come.

forever young and vibrant
Effortlessly energetic and lean-a practical
owner's manual for the body.

the currency of thought
Achieving universal wealthcare by identifying
how thoughts affect finances.

Welcome to the 'IN THE BEGINNING...*there was wellness*' series. The status of your health is always changing. Health is a continuum. The relevance of each of the books in the series depends on where you are in your health cycle. Are you sick? Are your children sick? Do you want to insure that your children have optimal health? If so, you are beginning with the right book, saving 'generation next'.

Once you understand the true source of illness, you will be ready to rediscover youth and vitality. A practical blueprint is not enough. What is needed is a true owner's manual for the body. Some people treat dandruff with Selson Blue not realizing that the true problem lies inside! Learn how to connect the dots in forever young and vibrant!

If you feel YOU are standing in the way of your dreams and you want to get 'unstuck', then read the currency of thought.

An introduction to the series, 'IN THE BEGINNING... *there was wellness*', appears at the beginning of each of Debi Waldeck's three books. If this is your second book of the series and you have already read the introduction, feel free to begin with Chapter one.

SERIES INTRODUCTION

Have you ever received truly bad news, the kind of news that grips your heart? It could apply to either you or someone you love. "You have cancer; you are suffering from major depression; you have fibromyalgia; or you are going to lose your home." The kind of things that knock you off your feet! I'm here to tell you that you can receive this type of news and you do not need to be afraid; you can get through it!

I was raised in the South and as I travel the world and share this message, I've come to realize that there's something unique about us Southerners. We think we can say anything, any old thing at all, as long as we start or end with blessing someone's heart. As in, "Did you see her hair, bless her heart?" Or, "Bless his heart, he takes such good care of his mama." So I want to tell you right up front that I am not going to hold back with you. You need information and you are ready for it! *Bless your hearts.* Raised a poor girl in the South, I learned that the real gold in life is knowledge. So let's just be honest and fast-forward to where you want your life to be.

Why do you indisputably accept the media's

information as gospel, or what the doctor says or what your boss says or even what your mother or father say? Aren't you in control of your life? That's really the big question here, isn't it? So take control! Start asking, "Who says so?" or "Why does someone else's reality have to be my reality?"

When I was a young adult, my doctor told me I had an autoimmune disease. It was very unusual at that time for someone my age to receive such a diagnosis. But I received the diagnosis and *I was afraid.* Then I was given a medication that, back then, wasn't known to cause any potential problems with an unborn child. Today, the *Physician's Desk Reference* recommends that women not take that medication if they plan to get pregnant... maybe because of people like me.

I will never know for sure whether the medication caused complications in my son. What I do know is that the doctor told us to "abort the baby" after he recognized complications. I asked. "Who says so?" Maybe I was in denial. Hey, I think denial can be a good thing at times! I thought, "We were created to be well, to be prosperous and to have peace of mind." I remembered those promises and I set out to achieve what I had been promised.

Imagine that you find a magic lantern. What would you ask for? When I was a little girl, and still to this day, I have asked for one thing: To see the world through the eyes of God. Well, be careful what you wish for—you just might get it! In my simple, childlike and innocent mind, I thought, "If God is all-knowing and God is in me, then I have access to all that is. It is a part of who I am." So from an early age, I heard messages from the world around me, but I became conditioned to check those external messages with "All That Is," that "Still Small Voice" inside of each of us that is always there if we will but listen. I learned to distinguish my own voice from "All That Is." Early in life, my prayers were never talking or pleading; instead my prayer was listening. Perhaps this is how *Debi's Dialogue* was born.

If you have a question on your heart or in your life, go to your quiet place and ask it. Take a notebook, listen and then write the answers that come to you. You may surprise yourself. After all, why must you constrain your thoughts by asking for everyone else's opinion?

You are about to embark on a journey with me. Some parts are autobiographical so you can see the external circumstances that led me to this journey. Some parts of this book are technical to educate you.

Start by asking yourself, "Is the society we have created what I desire?" Yes? If so, why are so many people in debt? Why do so many people barely scrape by, living from paycheck to paycheck? How can you commit to "All That Is" when "All that is" for you is worrying about how to pay the next bill?

Why are so many people obese or suffering with chronic health conditions such as asthma, high blood pressure, lupus, depression and more? Do you really believe our bodies were created without the ability to heal?

Some are becoming more enlightened and connected, while others are becoming less conscious, more asleep, more brainwashed that this truly is "as good as it gets." *You* don't fall into the latter category, of course, or you wouldn't have this book in your hand. *Bless your heart!*

I'll admit I was nervous about unveiling my innermost thoughts to you. However, I have chosen to see myself through God's eyes, not the eyes of man. So I will go forward into the unknown. I will either be carried or I will learn to soar. Either way, I will be okay and so will you. You are more powerful than you know; it can be frightening to be responsible for your power.

Do you want health,
wealth and peace of mind? I did.
Who could ask for anything more?

'IN THE BEGINNING...*there was wellness*' is the culmination of my 18 year journey. In this series, you will find a blueprint for physical, emotional and financial prosperity. If you are in a crisis, all you want at this point is to end the crisis. If you are currently in a health crisis, then you are not interested in Botox or achieving wealth. Your focus is to get out of your crisis by getting your health back. I know because I was in that place. I have spent at least ten-thousand hours researching the route and role of autoimmune diseases. I am here to share the profound relationship between wellness and absorption. If you have an autoimmune disease, depression or a child with ADHD, then you will enjoy this book, saving 'generation next' where we discuss the reasons behind the dramatic increase in autoimmune disease, autism and cancer.

I chose not to abort our son, Joshua, however, after birth, he suffered from various maladies including a significant heart defect. I voraciously studied nutritional principles through Joshua's first seven years of life. Yet, he was continually diagnosed with a new problem such as attention deficit disorder (ADD), respiratory airway disease, eczema and lazy eye. I was convinced that my autoimmune disease was not genetic since no one else in my family had ever been diagnosed. I was convinced that Joshua's problems stemmed from my autoimmune disease and the medication I was given. I did not want to sentence my son to a life of drugs and, more importantly, I did not want to thwart his personality. I wanted to know my son. For the first seven years of his life, I researched, tirelessly and ultimately, was able to apply the principles set forth in saving 'generation next'. Ultimately, we moved out of crisis. Once you're out of crisis, or if you do not have a health crisis, then your goal is to learn how to achieve optimal wellness, maintain what is good for you and slow the aging process. Would you like to slow the aging process? Who wouldn't? And doesn't everyone want to achieve optimal health and wellness?

When our crisis had passed, I found myself looking

for ways to maintain optimal wellness for my entire family. I discovered that optimal wellness comes first from changing our thoughts and then our lifestyle. I was ready to move toward achieving excellence. When you lose health, you wish to restore it, then maintain it and then improve it. In my second book, forever young and vibrant you will receive a practical blueprint for achieving and maintaining optimal health. You'll love this no-nonsense road map. Are you tired of too much information? Allow me to condense my ten-thousand hours of research into what's most important. I know you're tired of the latest magazine article, or that infomercial or the latest fad and just information overload in general. Then you go to the health food store, only to be bombarded with hundreds of products and even more information! Which product should you buy? Do you need to supplement your diet; can you get everything you need from your food? Does your eyesight really need to leave you when you turn 40? Finally, you'll have information you can use and have a true understanding of how your body works.

How many of us want peace of mind? How many of us want to create, rather than react? Reacting really slows you down. When you react, you are not living in the 'now'; you are living in the 'then'. In my third book, the currency of thought, you'll learn how to create and reprogram your self-talk and how to achieve your dreams. Excellence is not for the very few; it is for every one of us! I will also share how to balance family and work. Balance and excellence begins when we understand that the two most powerful words in the English language are "*I am*," as in "I am smart. I am funny. I am wealthy. I am fit. I am happy." Or, "*You* are smart. You are funny, you are wealthy, and you are fit." What do *you* want to be? Tell yourself! "*I am*_____" Then YOU fill in the blanks. Unfortunately, most people's "I am" statements are, "I am in debt" or "I am fat", "I am lazy", "I am tired" and so on. Little do people know that each utterance is programming the mind. In the currency of thought, you will learn how to change this dialogue.

As I moved from crisis to maintenance to excellence, I found I was ready to tackle money! Please, don't worry about money until you have "You" under control. I will share some short cuts to achieving financial excellence. But first, you need to understand the income you presently earn—is it permanent, or is it temporary? How do you create permanent wealth? What are your options when you have little time and money? Where are the trends when it comes to money or business opportunities? How about franchising or a college degree? You need to know I achieved financial success *only* after I had conquered the crisis, mastered optimal wellness and sought excellence.

The end of this story (or should I say the beginning) is that in 2008, Josh graduated with honors from his high school with an International Baccalaureate curriculum and has received a Congressional Appointment to attend the United States Military Academy known as West Point. This is the son who I was told to abort or, once being born, would have lived a life on pharmaceutical drugs. I did not listen! I asked why? I questioned the doctors and big pharma. I knew there had to be a better way. We are not designed to live on drugs; we are designed to be well.

KNOWLEDGE IS GOLD

Maybe it's important for me to share this information with you because early on, I realized the power of information. When I was a teenager we had little money. When I saw kids in school with their crisp white shirts, it prompted me to get baby sitting jobs so I could save my money and buy a can of spray starch.

I then spent hours ironing and starching my shirt to get that crisp, clean look. At school the next day, after sitting down for five minutes, there I was wearing a wrinkled, pathetic white shirt. It wasn't until I was 19 that I realized the kids with the shirts that looked like paper had gone to a professional cleaner. Something about not knowing that really ticked me off. Information is powerful, once you know how to get it.

Take a moment to jump-start your life because whether you have health challenges or not, every one of you knows someone who does. Read saving 'generation next'. For every one of you who wants to achieve optimal wellness (without becoming a fanatic along the way), read forever young and vibrant and for every one of you who dreams of a life of choices and time, then read the currency of thought, and let us laugh together!

*I believe in you. I believe in humanity. I believe
in our collective spirit. I believe we are greater
than our circumstances. I believe. Do you?
The choice is yours.*

Each book of the, 'IN THE BEGINNING...*there was wellness*' series offers you tools to help you navigate this blueprint for physical, emotional and financial success:

- Each chapter will conclude with *Debi's Dialogue*, a final thought summarizing each chapter.
- The more technical chapters will include a chapter summary and longevity tools.
- Throughout this series you will find the four "L" Principles:

- *Longevity Principles*
- *Laughter Principles*
- *Lifestyle Principles*
- *Leverage Principles*

- **52 Weeks to a Renewed You**

A workbook for those of you who have completed books one, two and three offering 52 exercises to adopt over the next year that will profoundly change lives.

Remember, every journey begins with a single step and with each step, you are successful and on your way!

DISCLAIMER

The following discussion is not intended to diagnose, cure, prevent or treat any diseases and these statements have not been evaluated by the FDA. In a decision issued Friday, January 15, 1999, the U.S. Court of Appeals for the District of Columbia ruled that the health claim rules imposed by the FDA are *unconstitutional and in violation of the Administrative Procedure Act.* The Court instructed the FDA to define "significant scientific agreement" for health claims on dietary supplement labels. The FDA is not allowed to cause me to suppress health claims outright as long as I include a disclaimer. The Court further held that four FDA Final rules (prohibiting certain nutrient disease relationship claims) are *invalid* under the First Amendment to the Constitution.

I am in full support of medications for crisis and acute illness. However, in this series I discuss the wisdom, or lack thereof, of living a life of 'managing' chronic health challenges with medications without first identifying the root cause. This series offers a stimulating discussion of the root of our health problems.

CHAPTER

1

The Beginning

In the Beginning, There Was Wellness

That statement alone could be controversial. What is "The Beginning" the statement begs to ask? Was "The Beginning" with Adam and Eve, Atlantis, the "Big Bang" or billions of years ago? I'll leave that question to the scientists and theologians. For the sake of this discussion, "The Beginning" to which I refer begins in the womb.

Many items you buy come with an instruction manual. When you buy a car, you are instructed as to what grade of oil and gas to use so the car will run optimally. You are told about how one system interacts with the next, for instance how the electrical system interacts with the fuel injection system. You have access to scores of books that tell you what to eat, how to exercise, or how to think positively and as Klemmer says, "if 'how to's were enough, we'd all be skinny rich and happy." So why aren't we? The reason we still struggle is because motivation does not come from a 'how to' book. Motivation to make change comes only when the pain of your current situation is greater than the pain of making a change and when you have a profound understanding of WHY taking the steps to make the change will benefit you. If you are not sure that the changes you are undertaking will really benefit you, it is difficult to stick to it. I was in that situation. I was in a place where I would lose my child unless I took steps to understand what was going on in my body and ultimately, in his. It is true that necessity is the mother of invention. I am going to share my struggle, pain and ultimate victory. Along the way, through my desire to save my children, I sought for why they were sick in the first place. After you read the three books in my series, you will truly understand why you get sick, how easy it is to make changes, how your entire body works and how one area affects the other. You will make changes because you understand why, not because I told you so.

Longevity, lifestyle, laughter and leverage begin with your health and the health of your children and carry on through the next generations. The information I am now revealing has dramatically improved the health of my family and those with whom I work. The information to which I refer is that from infancy, the "gut" trains the immune system. Improving the health of the intestinal area ultimately improves the overall immune system. In other words, a baby's gut matures properly with its initial inoculation from the mother, and then further with breast-feeding and its lifestyle.

Many people with chronic conditions say, "Well, it runs in my family." That may be true, but through my research, I discovered that genetics is only partly to blame. In the three generations since the Baby Boomers, our society's overall health has changed dramatically. You can't blame that entirely on genetics. Three generations will not create significant genetic changes!

Before you think of your own health, wealth and peace of mind—viewing your world globally— ask yourself: What about the next generation? Those who have yet to be born are referred to as, "Generation Next." I say this because a portion of your health today is a result of yesterday's generation.

Since it is very difficult to think positively when you truly feel lousy, I start my discussion in saving 'generation next' with how our immune system develops and the devastating effects when it is not developed properly... in the beginning. As I summarize how the immune system is developed in this chapter, it may seem complicated at first but, for the sake of your children, stick with it and understand that I will explain it fully in subsequent chapters.

THE FOUNDATION

After you finish this book, the following discussion will flow and be very easy for you to understand and you will remember that there are 10 bacteria in the body for every one cell. Bacteria are important! When a mother gives birth, the baby receives its first inoculation (maternal inoculation). During the birthing process, the baby swallows fluid from the mother's birth canal. This fluid teems with microbes that begin to grow and colonize along the infant's sterile intestinal wall. Microbes are bacteria. The intestinal wall is intimately related to the Gut-Associated Lymphoid Tissue (GALT). The GALT makes up 70% of our immune system. Therefore, the development of the intestinal area directly affects the immune system. When the baby is born and its intestinal wall is sterile; the GALT is thin and immature, as is the baby's immune system. Breast milk and proper colonization of beneficial bacteria in the gut ensures the maturation of the GALT and thus the immune system. I call this maternal inoculation the "first life," and that's why I use the phrase, "In the Beginning, there was wellness..." The "beginning" I refer to is birth and the first two years of life.

The quality of the intestinal bacteria is what "programs" the GALT and plays a role in *how* the immune system will function. The healthy GALT helps desensitize the immune system. However, with the huge increase in autoimmune disease and allergies, it is obvious the integrity of the GALT has been damaged; therefore, the immune

system becomes overly sensitive to many normally
non-threatening invaders, including food.
Additionally, toxins and undigested proteins can
enter the bloodstream and contribute to illness.

LONGEVITY PRINCIPLE #1
Gut bacteria affect the development of
the intestinal wall.

You may wonder why doctors don't talk about this.
Doctors think something along the lines of, "Yes,
I know if I give this medication, this antibiotic,
this steroid, etc., there will be a temporary
disruption in the intestinal bacteria because many
medications destroy both good and bad bacteria."
Some doctors may even suggest patients take yogurt
because yogurts sold in the United States contain
probiotics. But most yogurts are a poor source
of these good bacteria because the high amounts
of sugar they contain deactivate the probiotics.
However, I love Jaime Lee Curtis in the "Activia"
ads. I believe that daily supplementation with
products such as Activia and probiotics can be very

helpful. However, if you have health issues, you may need greater supplementation of probiotics. Doctors assume that even though there's a temporary disruption in intestinal bacteria, once patients are off the medication, their bodies will restore themselves. So along that same line, if you cut your finger, won't your body heal the cut in a matter of time, unless of course, you have an extreme immune challenge?

This way of thinking requires a huge assumption. To make the statement that the body will restore itself assumes the body is in balance in the first place. That leads us to the million-dollar question: *Can the body restore itself if it weren't in balance in the first place?* I propose that if the body *were* in balance, we wouldn't be at the doctor for chronic upper respiratory infections, sinus problems, allergies, asthma, autoimmune disease and even ADHD and some types of depression.

Making this assumption leads to another question: If we receive the healthy maternal inoculation during birth, why would our immune system become hyperactive? First, in order to get the maternal inoculation, our mother's birth canal needs to be abundantly populated with healthy and balanced microbial flora. Second, our initial inoculation is developed during breast-feeding and from our environment. Mothers' milk contains oligosaccharides which is a special sugar that actually ferments and acts as food for the initial inoculation of bacteria received during the birthing process. Oligosaccharides are also called prebiotics as they are necessary to grow probiotics that are considered beneficial bacteria. These special sugars actually protect and strengthen the immune system. Oligosaccharides are vital to the infant's maturing intestinal wall and hence the successful development of the baby's immune system.

LONGEVITY PRINCIPLE #2
Our first inoculation, or 'first life' DOES NOT come from a shot. It comes from our mothers during the birthing process and then from our food and environment.

This "first life," or maternal inoculation, drives and trains our immune system to respond appropriately to our environment. Ultimately, a well developed intestinal area and GALT will desensitize our immune system rather than sensitizing. A sensitized immune system is an overactive immune system and the result is increases in allergies, asthma, eczema, autoimmune disease, inflammation and more. Since many of the Baby Boomers were the first generation in history to miss out on their maternal inoculation when evaporated milk replaced breast milk, Baby Boomers had less of that "first life" to pass on to the next generation. What we're seeing now is that this dramatic change altered the health of the intestinal area and dramatically affected the Baby Boom generation's immune health—and consequently, that of future generations.

Baby gets what mother has, no better, no worse. Each generation is inoculated with the intestinal bacteria the mother has during delivery. At birth, we receive two kinds of inheritances: a genetic inheritance and a "microbial inheritance." Genes are a snapshot of who the mother and father were when they were born. On the other hand our "microbial inheritance," or that human inoculation, represents the mother's life, from her birth to the birth of her baby, not just the initial genetic blueprint. If Mom has a history of stress, or medication, or if she were not optimally maternally inoculated, then her inoculation is compromised. Again, Mom gives what she's got at the moment of her baby's birth—no more, no less.

The third way we get these beneficial bacteria is from a lifetime of inoculation as we are exposed to bacteria in our environment from our diet and even dirt! Some argue that when a child eats dirt, she is instinctively trying to improve the intestinal ecology. At the same time, we continually assault these bacteria with antibiotics—both in our diet and prescribed—stress, high sugar diets, chlorine, alcohol, food allergies and more. In addition, it is impossible to receive beneficial microbes from fruits and vegetables that have been irradiated. Many foods you eat have been exposed to radiation to destroy viruses, insects or microorganisms. When foods are exposed to radiation, they are called irradiated. Irradiation can be compared to pasteurization—heating liquids to kill pathogens (harmful proteins or bad bugs!). Fruits and vegetables contain components called fructooligosaccharides (FOS) that are similar to oligosaccharides found in breast milk.

Irradiation degrades fructooligosaccharides normally found in fruits. If a person were not breast-fed, had a life of medications, sugar or stress, then the immune system may be compromised and become hyperactive. Since fructooligosaccharides are prebiotics or fuel for our beneficial bacteria, then if you eat irradiated foods, you are not receiving an 'environmental inoculation' and may need to supplement with FOS.

PRESCRIPTION FOR DISASTER

If you look at the three generations to come along since the beginning of the Baby Boom, you'll find an interesting dilemma. Due to economics and refrigeration three generations ago, more than 50 percent of the Baby Boom generation were taken off of breast milk and given evaporated milk. At the time, evaporated milk was nothing more than cow's milk and sugar. (1) Around 1946, at the onset of the Baby Boom, women were told,

"Don't breast-fed; it is archaic. Give your baby this formula and this baby food." Refrigeration and the low cost of evaporated milk drove this campaign. For the first time in history, more than 50 percent missed out on a large portion of the secondary inoculation of good bacteria from mother's milk. (1) Instead, children received high sugar formulas and even cow's milk.

Children born during that time were probably born through abundantly populated birth canals, where they received their first inoculation of beneficial bacteria, but with no breast-feeding and the addition of sugars and cow's milk protein, how could the Gut Association Lymphoid Tissue develop properly? Moms of that day hadn't been exposed to situations that can diminish the beneficial bacteria of the gut, such as high sugar diets (we ate five pounds of sugar per year per person in the early 1900's and now eat as much as 148 pounds of sugar per year per person), chemicals, preservatives or overuse of medications such as antibiotics. Penicillin was only introduced in the U.S. in the late 1930's, so most moms of the 1940's had surely passed their childhood illnesses and hadn't received penicillin. Although beneficial, penicillin kills off both good bacteria and bad bacteria that exist not only in the birth canal, but in the intestinal area as well.

The Baby Boom generation grew up with penicillin, refrigeration, fast food, microwaves, chemicals and preservatives. Put it all together and you have a recipe for disaster that is now evidenced by increasing autoimmune disease, allergy, ADHD, autism and more. Baby Boomers received less of an inoculation due to not being breast-fed. Dietary and lifestyle factors such as a high sugar diet, soft drinks or an overuse of antibiotics further inhibited beneficial—and natural—inoculation.

Therefore, Baby Boomers were the first generation to experience a widespread reduction in the inoculation of beneficial bacteria. Those babies may have been born through an abundantly populated birth canal, but missed out on the rest of the inoculation from breast milk. They were fed the high sugar formulas and cow's milk which alters intestinal pH and allows pathogens or bad bacteria to grow, negatively affecting the GALT and immune system. Then those children grew up to be moms in the 60s and 70s who gave birth to babies through now deficiently inoculated birth canals and, for the most part, moms didn't breast-feed. High sugar diets were the norm and overexposure to antibiotics was becoming common. Children of the 60s and 70s grew up to have children of their own in the 80s, 90s and beyond. Today, mothers are having babies who are prescribed antacids at six weeks for chronic acid reflux!

LONGEVITY PRINCIPLE #3
We are being inadequately inoculated by our mothers. Due to our culture, mothers have less to give.

A baby's intestinal area needs to remain acidic. When the intestinal area is optimally populated with beneficial bacteria, known as probiotics or good bacteria, then these "acid loving" bacteria—produce acids which lower the pH of the intestines and effectively kill harmful pathogens like strep, staph or E. coli. Feeding the baby just one bottle of milk or giving the baby solid food too soon impedes the growth of the good bacteria and raises intestinal pH so that harmful organisms like E. Coli, strep and other pathogens can grow more readily. Evidence shows that over the last three generations, there has been a reduction in the quality of the inoculation of mother to baby creating a more alkaline state in the infant's intestines. Mothers who birth babies vaginally today and breast-feed can still produce infants that have an intestinal pH that is not acidic enough to prevent the growth of harmful pathogens due to three generations of a decline in maternal inoculation from mother to child. In preparation for birth, mothers want to address their own health and the health of their intestinal areas, which translates into how optimal the maternal inoculation will be for their babies.

EVIDENCE OF OUR ERRORS

There was a 56 percent increase in prescription antacids for children under age four from 2002 to 2006; in children age five to eleven, use of these drugs increased 31 percent during the same time. Could this be the reason for the 700 percent increase in prescriptions for ADHD and a 237 percent increase in autism in the last 12 years? (2, 3, 4) Since there is a profound relationship between wellness and absorption, the answer is, Yes! This is more than acid reflux. These are children with immature GALTs and immature immune systems that may be forever affected and never fully mature. The immature GALT increases oxidative stress and lowers glutathione levels, discussed more at the end of this book and more completely in forever young and vibrant. When the intestinal area is not properly developed, more toxins enter the bloodstream via the intestinal wall. All blood leaves the intestines and goes straight to the liver for cleansing. The liver now sees an increase in toxins and thus has more to filter. The increased filtration increases oxidative stress, depleting our bodies of precious stores of antioxidants, particularly glutathione. Research shows that autistic children, cancer patients and even diabetics have low glutathione levels. *The gut trains the immune system.* There is a profound relationship between absorption and wellness. This could be you—or your children.

Currently, the medical community has developed a definition of your health care from cradle to grave called the "continuum of care." The continuum of care is broken into five parts from primary or preventative care to palliative care—caring for those already sick—and then end of life care. The primary level in the continuum of care, or first care, begins with immunizations and vaccinations. My desire is that the series, IN THE BEGINNING... *There was Wellness* adjusts the definition of the continuum of care so the primary level will include first, maternal inoculations.

Many people want to blame our current sickness crisis on pesticides, chemicals, mold, silver fillings in the teeth, high power lines and so on. Although each of these factors may contribute, the key factor to your health is the strength of your immune system. Swine flu is looming and many will run for vaccinations. Each year, flu vaccinations miss the mark. What we should do is work diligently to improve the immune system by improving the health of the intestinal area and the GALT!

If you are not well, if you have allergies, migraines, eczema, depression, lupus or autoimmune disease, then you have an imbalance in the intestinal area. The imbalance negatively affects the optimal pH of the intestines and weakens the intestinal immune response resulting in a hyperactive immune system. Your gut trains your immune system.

Most who are sick or who have chronic illness have a compromised intestinal area leading to a compromised GALT, creating a hyperactive immune system. It is as though the roof is leaking, but we don't know it. All we know is there's water in the house. We're so busy changing the bucket (new diet, new drug, new fad, etc.) that we haven't thought to look at the roof (addressing the health of the intestinal area). In this book, you'll learn how to fix the roof!

Wake Up!

It is time to WAKE UP! It is time to ask questions. It is time for a little righteous anger for you are here to protect your children. My daughter has a friend whose mother is a doctor. I met the friend when she was fifteen years old. She had been diagnosed with juvenile rheumatoid arthritis (JRH) and evidence of the disease was already present as her arm was disfigured. I asked her 'what's up with your arm-bless your heart?" And she told me her story. She was born colicky, and put on antacids. At the age of four she was diagnosed with ODD or oppositional defiance disorder and put on meds. At the age of six, she was diagnosed with ADD or attention deficit disorder and put on Ritalin. At the age of eleven, she was diagnosed bipolar and put on Lithium. She then took out her pill box. This was not one of those 7 day pill boxes, it was a month pill box with 30 spots for pills... but these were her *DAILY* meds!! She was on Methotrexate (a chemotherapy drug) for her JRH. In fact, she was a mess. I shared with this teen the relationship between wellness and absorption. I suggested that being born colicky was an early sign that her intestinal area was out of balance. Since it was never resolved, her body was exposed to more toxins and chemicals early on since her intestinal wall did not develop properly and stayed thin and immature. Ultimately, this creates a hyperactive immune system which I will explain in detail later. Imagine a four year old with the intestinal integrity of an infant. What happens when they eat meat or cookies for instance, can you imagine feeding a newborn that way? Yet I will show you that her intestinal area is similar to a newborn's. This constant irritation is an extreme stress on the child. No wonder she was angry and had ODD. She was given drugs. Most medications reduce or alter stomach acid production, further affecting the integrity of the intestinal area. Yet that was what she was given. Next she was diagnosed with

ADD and she was given dexamphetamine. No wonder she became bipolar! In chapter 2 I will show you why this intestinal breakdown made her more prone to the JRH. How do I know her intestinal tract was negatively affected? The first evidence was the colic... but when I met her mother, it turned out that her mother had been given drops for her eyes as a teen. The drops contained a great deal of mercury. These drops were taken off the market but not before rendering the mother legally blind. Mercury is an extremely powerful antibiotic. It would have stripped the beneficial bacteria from the teen (the mother). With no knowledge that her body had been negatively affected, she gave birth to a baby who received very little beneficial bacteria that would have been passed along during the birthing process. If the mother fed the baby formula, she would deny the child oligosaccharides (the special sugars from mother's milk) and the baby was left with an immune system destined to be overactive.

If you or your children have several diagnoses and live on multiple medications I urge you to read this book to the end. You have the power to question authority. You are allowed to ask why! Why all the increase in dis-EASE? If it is all genetic then why are we seeing such a dramatic increase in autoimmune disease, depression, ADHD, autism and more? I don't plan to motivate you rather; I plan to irritate you into action for the sake of 'Generation Next." Most importantly, I want to give you your power back. Through this series, you will get to know 'you' on an entirely different level. It is time to get to know you. You are with your body 24 hours a day. You know the changes; you see yourself better than anyone. So, why do you listen without question or without thought to the opinion of another, even though they have medical training? I promise you, your doctor would do a better job if you would participate in the process by listening to your body, interpreting it and sharing it with him or her. There was a day when you went to the doctor with a slight sniffle and you were prescribed an antibiotic, when spending a week increasing the intake of fluids and chicken noodle soup would have done the trick. Now look at the effect prescribed antibiotics have had on our society with the rise of MRSA and super bugs. Today you go to the doctor with elevated cholesterol and are prescribed statin drugs, yet a high fiber diet, exercise and antioxidants would improve your numbers a great deal. Is it really true that our society is so lazy that we'd rather take a pill with known side effects then make a small change to live a happier and longer life? Maybe for others, but not for you.

What if today's babies and children actually do not have too much stomach acid? What if these babies are actually experiencing an extreme imbalance in the health of their intestinal tracts? What if people who are allergic don't just have "hyper" immune systems? What if their immune systems are responding to a hyper influx of toxins and undigested proteins that enter their bloodstreams through the intestinal tract? And further, what if their immune systems were never trained, due to the lack of healthy and balanced intestinal bacteria? What if the roof is leaking but we don't know it? All we know is that there's water in the house. But we're so busy changing the bucket (new drug, new diet, etc.) that we haven't thought to look at the roof. What if...?

DEBI'S DIALOGUE

Why do we resist change?
As Marianne Williamson said, "We are
afraid of our own power."

Why?
Because change gives you an opportunity
to know yourself, and people are afraid
to truly 'see' themselves.

Why?
Because people see themselves through
the eyes of all who have come
before them.

Sadly, people do not look at themselves
through the eyes of God because if they
did, they would stare all day long.

Why?
Because many people do not know God.

Why?

You start to know God when you learn to love yourself. To know God means you choose to love yourself exactly the way you are now - male, female, black, white, yellow, red, fat, skinny, ugly, pretty. The problem is that people seek man's approval before and above God's approval.

Why?

Because people have no faith. Faith is the opposite of fear. People are in fear and the cycle begins again.

Okay, everyone knows that faith is not fear. We know what it isn't, but what is faith?

Faith is to know that when you step into the unknown, you will not fall. You will either find your way or you will be carried. Faith is Trust.

What is Trust?

Trust is to know that you are loved.

But what if you have never been shown love?
It's the Man versus God thing again. Man must demonstrate love. To learn to trust, you must learn to love yourself. Only then will you come to know God.

Docs self-love remove God?
Don't worry that self-love takes God out of the equation.

**God does not need credit,
God needs to be demonstrated.**

CHAPTER

2

Prescription for an Autoimmune Disease

"Health is not valued till sickness comes."
~ DR. THOMAS FULLER (1654 - 1734), GNOMOLOGIA, 1732

An autoimmune disease is the result of the body attacking its own tissue as if it were something foreign. The result varies depending on the part of the body that is affected. For example, in multiple sclerosis, (MS), the body attacks the protective myelin sheath that covers the nerves much like the plastic coating on an electric wire. The nerve however looks different than a plastic wire. The protective covering on a nerve has gaps. Where there are gaps in the myelin sheath, the nerve looks rather like sausage links. The nervous impulse jumps from gap to

gap, speeding up the nerve conductivity. When
the myelin sheath is destroyed or frayed, more of
the nerve is exposed and the nervous impulse is
less efficient. Muscle weakening, atrophy (wasting
away) and paralysis can be the result. In rheumatoid
arthritis, the joints are attacked causing pain and
crippling deformity. In Crohn's disease, the gut
is attacked leaving it unable to fulfill its proper
function. The question is why?

After my diagnosis with an autoimmune disease
I began to wonder why there has been such
an increase in autoimmune diseases. Why has
there been such an increase in autism, ADHD,
depression, cancer and more? Is it genetic? As
far as I could tell from my research, no one in
my family had a history of autoimmune disease.
So, let's look at some highlights that led to the
diagnosis of *my* autoimmune disease and see if we
can find a trend.

My father went to Vietnam and after the war
ended our family experienced some financial
difficulties. We moved to Hampton, Virginia and
my father took various odd jobs for four years
until he found a position as a laborer at a nuclear

power plant. The odd jobs did not provide our family with health insurance and in the beginning of his career at the Surry Nuclear Power Plant we had only limited access to insurance. During this time, we really did not have a lot of money. I remember our family receiving free eyeglasses from the Lions Club. Do you remember as a child taking a can of food to school for the poor people at Thanksgiving? One Thanksgiving our family received a basket of food delivered to our door.

My mother is a meticulous woman. She grew up in modest conditions in Scotland, but she always said "We can afford soap and there is no excuse for being unkempt." Our shoes were always shined and our clothes were always pressed, though early on many came from Goodwill. My mother was and is an amazing woman. She was a rock during those difficult times always smiling and always making sure something hot was on our plate even if it were only a lot of potatoes or white bread covered in meat juice. No matter how little we had, my parents made every event seem special. They did the best they could. My mother had us brush our teeth in the morning and at night. She told us to brush our hair from root to end each day to release the natural oils, and she took us in for checkups when we could afford them. The doctors told my mother we were each as healthy as a horse.

I had no health problems until I was 15. By then, our insurance coverage was more complete and we were able to go to the dentist for the first time in a while. My mother walked into the dentist with four children, an insurance card and money for the co-pays. Even though I was just a child, I could see the dollar signs in the dentist's eyes. Before you know it, the dentist claimed that I had 15 cavities! I'd never had a cavity before that day and have not had one in the last ten years. Yet I had 15 cavities that day! I question to this day if I really had 15 cavities.

The dentist filled all 15 cavities in one day.

There is much controversy over whether silver fillings in teeth are harmful. The American Dental Association states that amalgam fillings rarely cause health issues, unless a person has preexisting sensitivities to mercury or nickel. In the opposing camp, many dentists believe amalgam fillings leach harmful mercury and metals into our bodies so they refuse to use them. Mercury is a powerful antibiotic. In a June 5, 2008 article in *Pregnancy News*, FDA spokesperson, Peper Long stated that the FDA will state a position on amalgam fillings by July of 2009. A notice on the FDA web site states, "Dental amalgams contain mercury, which may have neurotoxic effects on the nervous systems of developing children and fetuses."(1)

Regardless, no dentist I have spoken to since then would put 15 fillings in a teenager's mouth in *one day*. What I can tell you from my personal experience is that within three months of having the fillings, my face broke out in awful, painful cystic acne; I gained 30 pounds; I was extremely lethargic; I developed a chronic upper respiratory infection that put me out of school for almost a month and I slept all of the time. This was horrible for a teen approaching her "Sweet Sixteen" birthday!

My mother took me to a doctor who blamed my symptoms on puberty, although I had started puberty four years earlier! My doctor did not know me. I was just a case study. For the acne, he put me on an antibiotic called tetracycline.

I took the medicine for *18 months.* However, I have looked back and wondered whether the 15 fillings in one day created toxicity that affected my thyroid and caused it to slow down. The now slowed thyroid contributed to the weight gain and lethargy. From ages 16 through 18, I tried a myriad of fad diets and even starvation. Finally, as I approached my eighteenth birthday, I'd started to study nutrition and exercise and by the time I turned 18, I had my weight under control.

I went off to college and in my sophomore year, I was diagnosed with a duodenal (small intestinal) ulcer and put on prescription Tagamet, which is an antacid. I took that for 18 months. During this time, I was married. Our first child, Morgan, came eight weeks early. I had just started Lamaze classes and at the first session, they told us, "When your time is close, you'll have a *show*," (a release of the mucus plug that protects the infant by sealing the cervix). Well, I'd already had my "show" earlier that day, but because I was so young, when I tried to tell my doctor about it, he didn't take me seriously. That was June 26, 1986.

On Sunday, June 29, while I sat in church, I

experienced a huge kick that felt like my daughter was going to come right out of me. I immediately knew something was wrong. Remember, though, we still had eight weeks until she was due. So on Monday, June 30, I went to my OB/GYN, and upon examination, he found that Morgan had put her tiny foot through my cervix. She was so small that she didn't even break my water. Of course, she was in the breach position—feet first. They would have to perform a C-section. The doctor said he would schedule it for the next day. I told him I didn't think I could wait, but who was I? I was so young; I didn't know anything, and he sent me away.

I lived an hour away from the doctor and was extremely uncomfortable. I went to my Mom's home instead, since she lived 20 minutes from the hospital. The second I walked in the door, I immediately went into labor. My mother, a timid five foot tall Scottish woman, got on the phone with my doctor. She chewed him out and made sure I'd be seen that day! Later that afternoon at 5:25 p.m., they performed an emergency C-section because Morgan's heart rate was dropping and the umbilical cord was around her neck.

Our daughter was eight weeks premature. Her lungs were intact, but she had an immature digestive tract. She spent her first weeks in an incubator because she had an elevated bilirubin count. Bilirubin is the by-product of red blood cell metabolism. Normally bilirubin is secreted in the bile (the yellow stuff seen in vomit) and is broken down by bacteria in the gut. Since Morgan was so premature and since she was born via C-section, she did not have enough gut bacteria to break down the red blood cell by-product. In an infant, bilirubin can pass the blood brain barrier, which is also immature, and cause neurological problems. The blood brain barrier is a physical barrier that protects our brain from harmful chemicals and toxins. Morgan's skin was yellow and she was put under a special light in the incubator that helped clear the bilirubin. But it wasn't over since her red blood cell count was dropping. They told us that my body had sent out antibodies to kill off her red blood cells. This was not normal. I asked why, but it seemed my understanding the situation was not their first priority. They scheduled Morgan for a total blood transfusion at the Children's Hospital of the Kings Daughters in Norfolk, Virginia.

In 1986, the thought of AIDS was new and scary. Many of my family had O+ blood type, known as the "universal donor" since type O blood people can only receive O blood, but O blood can be safely given to all other blood types. My family lined up to give blood to avoid any risk of Morgan getting AIDS. Just as the hospital was set to perform the procedure, Morgan's tiny body began to out produce the red blood cells that the antibodies from my body had been attacking. And just like that, the transfusion was no longer necessary. I wish I had known then that this situation might have been an early warning sign of my over reactive immune system and impending diagnosis of an autoimmune disease.

After Morgan's birth, my heart rate gradually increased. At its peak, my resting heart rate was 156 beats per minute. Imagine, 156 is probably your target heart rate in an aerobic class, not while sitting watching television! I went to the doctors numerous times after Morgan's birth with feeling of anxiety and vision disturbances. I was told to 'get a grip on my type A personality' and prescribed a tranquilizer. How many of you would just do as the doctor said? I never filled the prescription, because I knew my body and I knew it was changing. My hands shook all the time and at one point a doctor accused me of taking illegal drugs. When I spoke with people, I had two conversations going on in my head at the same time, one was what you heard out loud and the other was me saying to myself, "slow down, calm down, you're freaking them out!" One of my clients noticed my symptoms and suggested I get my thyroid checked. Finally, two years after Morgan was born and with a heart rate of 156, I was diagnosed with Graves' disease. Graves' is an autoimmune disease that causes a hyperactive thyroid and overproduction of thyroid hormone. I asked, "Why do I have Graves' disease?" I was told it was genetic. Since I now know that our immune system is intimately connected to our intestinal area, here is what I think:

1. 15 fillings in one day disrupted the good bacteria in my gut and negatively affected my thyroid.
2. 18 months of tetracycline further negatively affected the good bacteria in my gut.
3. 18 months of Tagamet further created an imbalance of the good bacteria in my gut.
4. My intestinal wall was damaged and this

affected my Gut Associated Lymphatic Tissue (GALT).

5. The disrupted GALT negatively affected my immune system.

6. My immune system became overactive, predisposing me to an autoimmune disease.

7. I may have gotten Graves' disease because I was genetically predisposed to it, but the trigger was the hyperactive immune system. In you, it could be MS, rheumatoid arthritis, Crohn's, and so on.

LONGEVITY PRINCIPLE #4
Genetic predispositions do not have to dictate your future.

Through this book, you'll learn that many "minor" maladies that may plague you are actually red flags that your immune system is compromised. Have you or any of your friends received diagnoses of chronic fatigue, depression, fibromyalgia, lupus, cancer and more? Can we agree that the immune system may be involved? What if minor maladies such as chronic headaches, eczema, asthma or allergies are a red flag that your intestinal area is out of balance, your GALT is immature and you are subject to a hyperactive immune system that can put your health in jeopardy?

Without the stimulation of a baby and with Morgan in an incubator, my body couldn't produce breast milk. Since Morgan was born C-section, she missed the initial inoculation not being born through the birth canal nor swallowing the fluid. Even if Morgan was born vaginally, I doubt she would have gotten much of an inoculation since I had been on antacids which reduce stomach acid, antibiotics which alter gut bacteria and the 15 fillings in one day which assaulted my entire system. Since Morgan was in the incubator, I was unable to feed her the special sugars from breast milk that could have helped develop her intestinal area and train her immune system. Her first months and years were filled with trips to the doctor for antibiotics for chronic sinus problems. She had her tonsils removed, and she suffered from leg cramps, anxiety and more. Today she is a very strong and determined young lady, largely as a result of the discoveries you will find in this book. At one time, Morgan was extremely lactose intolerant. Today, she can consume milk, cheese or ice cream with no digestive or sinus issues. I predict, based on the research presented in this book, that Morgan never lacked the lactase enzyme rather her intestinal pH was so alkaline that it 'turned off' the lactase enzyme making her appear lactose intolerant. As we corrected her intestinal pH, her naturally occurring lactase enzyme now works and she can now tolerate dairy products. I often wonder what would have happened to her if she hadn't "kicked" her way out. Would she have been stillborn as my body sent antibodies to attack her red blood cells? What would have happened to her overall health without the discoveries we made together? Would she be forever sick?

After Morgan was born my monthly menstrual cycle did not resume. When I asked my doctor about the risks of amenorrhea (not having a period), he responded that I should be happy—no mess! In the months that followed Morgan's birth, my heart rate steadily increased until it peaked at 156 beats per minute, another sign that something was wrong with my immune system. Both were symptoms of my impending autoimmune disease diagnosis.

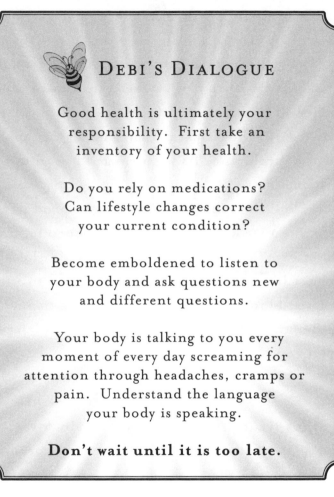

DEBI'S DIALOGUE

Good health is ultimately your responsibility. First take an inventory of your health.

Do you rely on medications? Can lifestyle changes correct your current condition?

Become emboldened to listen to your body and ask questions new and different questions.

Your body is talking to you every moment of every day screaming for attention through headaches, cramps or pain. Understand the language your body is speaking.

Don't wait until it is too late.

3

A Letter to Michael

"I'm looking at the man in the mirror, I'm helping him to change his ways. I'm looking at the man in the mirror, If you want to make the world a better place, Take a look at yourself and make a change."
~ MICHAEL JACKSON

Recently, Superstar Michael Jackson died. I was very saddened because I always wanted to have this conversation with him regarding his lupus and vitiligo - both are autoimmune diseases.

Michael, I think I know why you feel bad and were diagnosed with lupus and vitiligo. You have been a star since the age of five. Money was flowing in. You could have anything you wanted so you asked for soda and sweets and because your mom could afford to give it to you, she gave it freely. Now

Michael, I do not know if you were breast-fed or about the health of your mother, but I would guess as fantastic as your stardom seemed to us on the outside, for you it was grueling and stressful. You are a perfectionist and you understand the music like few others. Some time ago, you began to wear a glove. I suspect Michael, it was because of the fungus that you had on your fingernails. How do I know that? A few years ago I watched a documentary about you and I saw your grey fingernails and soda in many of the shots of you. Michael, the fungus on your nails was a sign that your intestinal area was out of balance years ago and the stress and sugar was weakening your intestinal wall. Over time, food proteins and proteins from viruses and bacteria were able to enter your immune system by passing through your now damaged intestinal wall. As these proteins entered your bloodstream and were 'seen' by your immune system, your body began to produce antibodies. An antibody is produced when a protein is identified as foreign. For you Michael, your immune system saw your own melanin as foreign, attacked it and you had vitiligo or patches of white on your skin. The glove on your hand may also have been an attempt to hide these new vitiligo spots. I suspect Michael that being on a stage with all the lights, you could not tolerate patches of white skin marking your gorgeous chocolate skin, so you did what you had to do, you lightened all your skin to mask the vitiligo. But Michael, because you never fixed the root issue, the imbalanced intestinal area, the proteins continued to flood your immune system and your body continued to create antibodies. Eventually the antibody mistook your own body as foreign and you developed lupus. By the way Michael, it is not uncommon for people who have severely imbalanced intestinal areas to have insomnia because it is difficult to absorb minerals when the intestinal area is damaged. Deficiencies in magnesium, calcium and potassium mean your body or your muscles cannot relax and it is difficult to sleep. Your mind races and you wake always feeling tired. Michael, let me explain how an autoimmune disease works.

WHAT IS AN ANTIGEN?

When a protein in the body is identified as foreign or 'non-self', an immune response results, the protein is now identified as an antigen and it is attacked. The body's immune system is designed to seek out harmful proteins and destroy them. However since we are made of proteins, it is important that our immune system is working properly so that our body tissue is not mistakenly attacked, such as in MS, type I diabetes or rheumatoid arthritis. A foreign protein may come from food that is not completely digested, or the protein may come from parts of a virus or bacteria. When your body sees the protein or antigen and recognizes it as foreign or a threat, it creates an *antibody* that will attack the "tagged" protein. The word antigen originated from the idea of *anti*body *gen*eration. Often, the "attack" creates inflammation or a histamine response. In the worse case, the antibody response produces an autoimmune disease. A protein or antigen is made of amino acids. In fact, a protein is hundreds of amino acids long; so how would an antibody "tag" a protein that needs to be attacked? This is very important, because the body is made of proteins and we do not want our immune system attacking our own body tissue. When the body attacks self, the result is an autoimmune disease.

WHAT IS AN ANTIBODY?

Why would the body, in its infinite wisdom, attack itself? This is a simplistic discussion of a complicated process, but will be helpful as we discuss autoimmune disease. There are 20 different types of amino acids. Proteins are long chains of amino acids. Imagine a combination on a lock that is 196 numbers long that can be one of 20 different numbers. Let's say a specific protein is made of 196 amino acids. The protein may look like: 1, 5, 8, 11, 20, 15, 6, 4, 2, 3, 8, 3, 16......4, 6, 18, 17 or 196 different numbers. The only difference is rather than numbers, the amino acids have names like lysine, valine, glutamic acid, arginine and more. Therefore, a protein will be hundreds of amino acids long, and each of the amino acids will be one of twenty different amino acids. Imagine the complexity if you were to memorize the combination of a lock that is 196 numbers long and each number is 1-20? Chains of these amino acids are called polypeptides and chains of polypeptides make up a protein. You can see how large it is. So to produce an antibody to attack a protein could be very difficult if the antibody had to know the exact "combination of the lock." In the efficiency of the body, rather than memorize the entire 'combination,' the immune system looks for a small sequence of amino acids within the combination. An antibody says to itself, "Ah ha! When I see the sequence of amino acids *20, 15, 6, 4, 2* or valine, proline, glutamic acid, aspartic acid and arginine, then I will attack it." You can see how much more efficient this is as opposed to trying to "remember" the entire sequence of 196 amino acids. The body only "tags" a small sequence of amino acids that make up the protein rather than the entire combination in the protein.

Later in this book, we will discuss some reasons why the body makes this mistake. All I know is that my thyroid had slowed and I became sensitive to iodine; then my body produced an antibody that looked like thyroid stimulating hormone and my thyroid began to overproduce and I felt crazy, sleeping two hours, losing weight and so hyper I scared people. Mind you, mercury is a powerful antibiotic as is tetracycline. Do you think, maybe, just maybe, the mercury in those amalgam fillings and the 18 months of tetracycline helped strip the beneficial bacteria from my intestinal area? Did this upset the balance in my small intestine leading to an ulcer?

Since the gut trains the immune system, do

you think, maybe, just maybe, the resulting breakdown in the health of my intestinal area could have affected my GALT thereby affecting my immune system? As we will discuss later, the original purpose of the GALT is to teach the immune system to be *desensitized* to its surrounding environment rather than be *hypersensitive* to it as is the case in allergy and autoimmune disease.

ASK YOURSELF

Do you think, maybe, just maybe, the resulting inability to break down proteins properly with the prescription antacid (Tagamet reduces acid production), could have resulted in undigested proteins and toxins being able to enter my bloodstream via the now damaged intestinal area? Remember, when the body sees a foreign protein, the body will create an antibody to "tag" the protein as an invader and attack it, which results in an increase in antibodies now attacking these "foreign proteins." The more damaged the intestinal area, the less developed the GALT. The more damaged the intestinal area, the greater the numbers of proteins that are able to enter the bloodstream. The less developed the GALT, the more hyper sensitive the immune system.

The more antibodies the body makes, the more opportunity for autoimmune disease. Once again, the gut trains the immune system.

What if the sequence of amino acids on the protein from a food or virus is the same sequence of amino acids on some part of you, for instance, your myelin sheath or your synovial sac surrounding your joints? Unfortunately, sometimes the sequence of amino acids that is "tagged" can look like our own tissue and the body mistakenly attacks us or "self." Would the increase in proteins entering the blood stream from an intestinal area that is not in balance increase the opportunity for autoimmune disease? This was a question I set out to answer. The change in our GALT, in our intestinal health and in our infants' intestinal pH has contributed to the increase of chronic illnesses. Do you really think it's all genetic?

The intestinal area is exposed to more foreign proteins on any given day than the immune system will see in a lifetime. In the creation of our body, the intestinal area was designed with an understanding that the intestinal wall is the real barrier between the 'outside' and 'inside' of us, much like our skin protects our insides. It is hard to believe but the intestinal tract is actually on the outside of us. Don't be fooled that once you eat the apple and it disappears as you swallow, that the apple is inside you. The nutrients of the apple are not inside of you until they are digested, assimilated and absorbed and then enter your bloodstream. However, when the intestinal tract is compromised, then the immune system unfortunately is exposed to more foreign proteins and the risk for autoimmune disease increases.

NO WORRIES, NO MESS

During the two years that my heart rate was increasing, I went to the doctor numerous times; no menstrual cycle—no worries, no mess! I had migraines, anxiety, restlessness—no worries. They prescribed a tranquilizer (I never filled it) and suggested some classes to "Handle my Type-A personality!" It was more than a Type-A personality; it was symptoms of an overactive thyroid from my Graves' disease that was yet to be diagnosed and caused me to sleep three hours, eat every two and get irritated because no one else could keep up. I felt like Wonder Woman on crack! My poor husband; I remember later seeing commercials about anxiety attacks and thinking, "Oh, that's what that was!" I thought I was psychic because I continually had feelings of impending doom. It wasn't just once that I called members of my family in a panic to make sure they were safe before I felt any relief. All of this was from symptoms of Graves' disease.

When I finally had my diagnosis of Graves' disease, I was actually relieved because now we could do something about it, right? Wrong! There is no cure for an autoimmune disease, only ways to manage the symptoms. Have you ever wondered why there has been such an increase in attention deficit disorder, or autoimmune diseases like multiple sclerosis, rheumatoid arthritis, Crohn's disease or how about cancer?

Some say we've become better at diagnosis. If that's the case, since there are few tests to screen children, why has there been an increase in neurological disorders, autoimmune disease and cancer even in our children? If it's all genetic, then why has chronic illness quadrupled since 1970 in our children (1)? Is it *all* genetic? Genetics are certainly important, but genetic predisposition is like being born with a loaded pistol in your pocket. What you do in life oftentimes determines whether you pull that trigger or not.

An article was published called Trends in Autism Prevalence: The Kids Are Alright, which is a statistical look arguing that our kids are no sicker today than 30 years ago.(2) I was alarmed at the discussion stating that neither depression nor illnesses have increased that would affect activity. If that is so, then how do we explain the dramatic increase in prescriptions to our children for depression, asthma or hyperactivity? It is time to explain the soaring increases in chronic health conditions in our country.

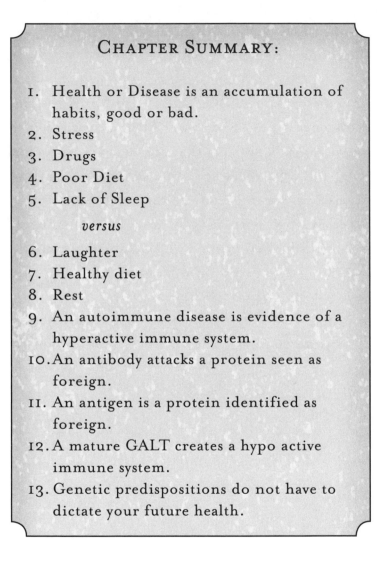

Chapter Summary:

1. Health or Disease is an accumulation of habits, good or bad.
2. Stress
3. Drugs
4. Poor Diet
5. Lack of Sleep

   versus

6. Laughter
7. Healthy diet
8. Rest
9. An autoimmune disease is evidence of a hyperactive immune system.
10. An antibody attacks a protein seen as foreign.
11. An antigen is a protein identified as foreign.
12. A mature GALT creates a hypo active immune system.
13. Genetic predispositions do not have to dictate your future health.

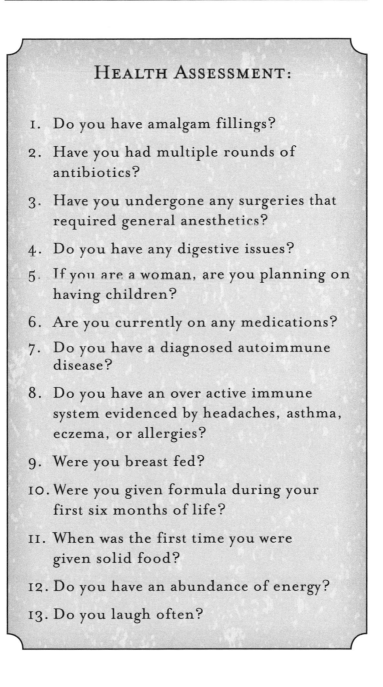

HEALTH ASSESSMENT:

1. Do you have amalgam fillings?

2. Have you had multiple rounds of antibiotics?

3. Have you undergone any surgeries that required general anesthetics?

4. Do you have any digestive issues?

5. If you are a woman, are you planning on having children?

6. Are you currently on any medications?

7. Do you have a diagnosed autoimmune disease?

8. Do you have an over active immune system evidenced by headaches, asthma, eczema, or allergies?

9. Were you breast fed?

10. Were you given formula during your first six months of life?

11. When was the first time you were given solid food?

12. Do you have an abundance of energy?

13. Do you laugh often?

DEBI'S DIALOGUE

What would happen if you were given the keys to a car in another country and never any instructions on how to drive or the rules of the road? You would careen through an intersection and get into an accident because you had no idea what the red octagonal sign means.

Our culture needs a rules book for the body. It is INSANE to mask headaches, cramps, pain, acid reflux, sleeplessness, anxiety and more with a medication without addressing the reason for the symptoms in the first place!

There is an accumulative value in investing small amounts of energy towards your health.

Over an extended period of time, your accumulative efforts, whether positive or negative, will have a corresponding effect on your health. Each day, you become healthier or sicker.

The choice is yours.

Choosing to Believe

"Never deprive someone of hope: it might be all they have."

~ H. Jackson Brown Jr.

I often laugh that God must think me really "slow" or dim-witted because my experiences were somewhat dramatic and therefore, easy to recall and document. You may not have had my experiences, those of my daughter's friend, or Michael's, however, you may have received an inadequate inoculation from your mother. You may be under chronic stress; you may be on medications that disrupt your intestinal tract and you may have been raised on a high sugar diet filled with chemicals and preservatives. I don't know, but I do know that many individuals suffer with an intestinal area that is out of balance, thus negatively affecting the immune system.

I was diagnosed with Graves' disease in November 1988. The doctor put me on medication to slow my thyroid. In January 1989, I became pregnant with our second child. I was elated! We were a little more secure in our jobs. I could actually have a nursery for this baby, even though we didn't have much money. At my young age, the first pregnancy had been somewhat stressful, yet I was very excited to be expecting now.

By March 1989, I had been on thyroid suppressing medication for five months and I had been pregnant eight weeks. I began to have pain and I began to hemorrhage so I was rushed to the same OB/GYN who had delivered Morgan almost three years earlier. They did an ultrasound. It was an interesting experience. With my first pregnancy, the nurse had "oohed and ahhed" over the baby's heartbeat and such during the ultrasound. But this time, the nurse didn't say a word. There was no talking. Instead, the nurse put down the scope and said, "The doctor will be right in to see you."

When the doctor came in, he didn't look at me. Instead, with his glasses perched at the end of his nose, he flipped through my file and said, "We're going to schedule you for a D&C this afternoon." I was confused and asked "what is a D&C?" The doctor explained how the lining of my uterus would be scraped. D&C means dilation and curettage. In essence, they were scheduling me for an abortion.

Time stood still as I contemplated the impact of his words. I felt weightless, absent from my body. I wanted this baby. Our daughter had been born eight weeks premature and by C-section. I had to leave my baby at the hospital in an incubator. I'd gone for a haircut the day I left the hospital, and I remember thinking that the girl cutting my hair had no idea that three days earlier, I'd had my first child. I was determined never to go through anything like that again.

I told the doctor no. He became incredibly agitated and told me if I did not have the D&C, I would have a physically malformed or mentally deficient child, or I would probably be back in the hospital in a few days with a fever from an infection, because what he saw looked like it was five days, not eight weeks, gestation. Well, Elvis left the building! I walked out with the weight of his words hanging over me. At the time we lived in Chesapeake, Virginia. My husband had been with a defense contractor, but when they lost the contract, he took a position with a bank in Richmond, Virginia and was gone four days a week. When I received the news from the doctor, I was alone and I felt so isolated. Who could help me make this decision? Have you ever felt this way?

Funny how at times like this, most everyone prays. When I arrived home that day, I walked into the bedroom, fell on my knees and began to pray. "Father, help me accept this." But the moment those words rolled off my lips, *I knew there was no truth to this.* I knew it was not God's will for me to have a mentally deficient or physically malformed child. The second that *awareness* penetrated my spirit, I felt as if a comforting blanket fell across my shoulders. In that moment, I felt instant peace. I heard, "You will have a healthy baby boy, and his name will be Joshua Daniel." It was so real to me that I said out loud, "Well, you need to tell John, because he wants to name his son John, Jr."

At that moment, I stood up, and it was finished. It was done. I cannot describe exactly what happened to me that day, but I got more than a healing. It was the gift of faith. But like any gift, I had the choice of whether or not to receive it.

Has anyone ever given you a compliment and you just shrugged it off? Has anyone ever offered you assistance in time of need and you said no? The only difference with me was I chose to believe the promise given to me that day. I chose to receive the gift and to be forever grateful. And I knew with more certainty than I know my name that my son was whole, and I knew his name.

Can it be that simple; can it be a function of choice? The Bible tells us that when Mary, the mother of Jesus, met Elizabeth, the mother of John the Baptist, Elizabeth was already with child and her baby leapt for joy within her womb at the recognition of Jesus within the womb of Mary. Elizabeth was further along in her pregnancy, and Mary had just become pregnant with Jesus.

What is interesting about this story is that Elizabeth didn't say, "Awesome Mary; you are the mother of the Son of God!" or "Wow, Mary; you are carrying God!" No, she said, "Blessed Mary, are you; for you have chosen to believe the promise of God." (Luke 1: 39-43)

I am sure a lot of people won't like what I am about to say... Bless their hearts, but... What if God went to many people with the promise, but only Mary chose to believe? What if God went to many people and told them to build an Ark, but only Noah was crazy enough to believe? What if God showed many people they could change the world like Ghandi or Mother Teresa but only a few heeded the call? How many people were shown a vision of impacting our society and went on to host a TV show that millions would see, but only a few, for instance, Oprah, chose to believe?

What if some are not more special than others?
What if we are all chosen—but only
some choose to believe?

LAUGHTER PRINCIPLE #1
A gift has no value until it is opened and accepted.

Two days later, when I went to the hospital for an ultrasound, my bleeding had become spotty. Then the technician showed me the baby's *heartbeat*. Yes! A heartbeat! I was told to find a local OB/GYN. The doctor who'd delivered our daughter lived more than an hour away. I'd only gone to my original doctor because I was afraid. I knew I should find a local OB/GYN. I learned that the bleeding made for an at risk pregnancy. I found a local doctor and once the bleeding subsided, I pursued a normal prenatal routine.

Three uneventful months later, on May 6, 1989, the day after my birthday, my husband, daughter and I spent the day with my parents in Norfolk at a Greek Festival. I was five months pregnant and I felt great. When we got home that evening, I stood inside the screened front door and my husband and father stood on the other side of the door on the front porch. Suddenly, I felt as if I were wetting my pants and when I looked down, I saw blood, so much blood! I gasped and my husband and father turned and saw the same thing. The blood spread rapidly across the bottom of my white shorts and my white sandals captured the falling blood.

Looking back, what's interesting is that no one even asked what was wrong. It was instant action! My husband quickly put me in the car and we raced to the hospital. I tried to hold in the blood, like you would do if you had to go to the bathroom. I somehow thought this was some kind of urinary tract infection. I found out later I was wrong.

When we got to the emergency room, once again, no one asked what was wrong or for my insurance information or anything like that. Instead, they whisked me back to a room where the nurses and doctors got to work. They took my blood pressure and saw it was falling so they put in an IV to re-hydrate me and improve my blood pressure. The nurses kept putting a blue absorption pad under me, but it filled with blood so rapidly they were continually changing it. We waited on this Saturday night for the ultrasound tech to come in and find out what was wrong. They told me I was losing the baby.

When the tech came in, she rubbed her hands together and said, "Alrighty then, let's see what we have here; probably a baby with a heart on the outside. There is a reason you're trying to lose this baby."

LAUGHTER PRINCIPLE #2
Sometimes even the smartest people with the best intentions are wrong.

I was catheterized and they began. After several anxious moments, the tech said, "Well I don't know why you are trying to lose this baby, but *he* looks okay." And with that, I had my first confirmation that this in fact was Joshua Daniel! The tech said it looked like I had a placenta previa and that it was an at risk pregnancy. She explained that the placenta was lying atop my cervix and the risk was that I could have the baby prematurely. Therefore, they said I needed complete bed rest for the reminder of my pregnancy. Later, when my blood pressure stabilized, I was released from the hospital.

I learned very quickly that it's virtually impossible to have total bed rest when you have a daughter who's almost three years old. So within ten days, I was up and about, although I did take it easy. On Wednesday, May 17, I decided to ignore the "total bed rest" advice and go to church with my mother. I believed the promise I would have a healthy baby boy, but I think I needed a little confirmation. There was an altar call that night for healings. I thought maybe I should go down and get some *reassurance*, so away I went. They took us into the prayer room and a church elder took my hands and prayed with me. At that moment, I once again felt as if I were wetting my pants. I rushed to the bathroom, where I passed a blood clot that was so big, it could have fit in both of my hands. It looked more like a liver than anything. The problem was I had no idea what had happened. I was young and again, very scared and confused. I came out of the bathroom to where my mother stood waiting for me. She told me I looked like I had seen a ghost and I said, "Please, just take me home."

Have you ever felt overwhelmed? Have you ever felt afraid? Somehow, with the healing I received in March I also found I did not react like another would in this situation. It was almost as if I was simply watching a movie. I was not afraid because I knew the outcome. Regardless of what the doctors said, I was going to have a healthy baby boy and his name would be Joshua. If we could only adopt that attitude in all things we would find our dreams and desires far less out of reach. Hold on to your ultimate desires and no matter what the current circumstances look forward to the promise (even one you make to yourself) with sweet anticipation.

I decided I would simply rest in God's promise that I would have a healthy baby boy and his name would be Joshua Daniel. But I admit I was tired. With the need for bed rest, I couldn't attend church regularly, so I began to pray a great deal. Somehow, after I passed that blood clot (or whatever it was), I felt very strong. On Thursday night, October 19, 1989, at full term, I delivered a fat, pink eight pound, fifteen ounce little man, named Joshua Daniel Waldeck. He was not early, he was not in an incubator and he was in my arms.

It was the happiest day of my life.

I reveled in the promise I'd received in March that I would have a healthy baby boy. Unfortunately, on Saturday, the doctor came into my room for what I thought would be a routine discharge from the hospital. Instead, he told me the nurse had found that Joshua had a heart murmur and they were calling in a cardiologist. Joshua would stay in a special ward for the night and the cardiologist would arrive in the morning. They said I could go home, but after what we'd gone through with Morgan, I said no way! So I became a hospital guest, no longer a patient.

As a "guest," you stay on another floor and no one comes to bring you water or check on you. Wow! What a difference. The good news is the nurses let me stay in the special ward and I held Joshua all night. When the cardiologist came the next morning, he examined Josh and told us he had a heart defect—a hole in his heart. Some holes are small and no real concern and some are larger. Joshua's was larger. The hole was a large ventricular septal defect (VSD). The heart has four chambers, the bottom two are the largest chambers and are called ventricles. In between the two ventricles is a wall. Josh had a hole in this wall. In the right ventricle is blood that has returned from the body and is low in oxygen; you may remember from your science books, that the blood is blue and represents low oxygen levels. This blood normally goes into the lungs for oxygen and ends up in the left ventricle rich with oxygen where it is then pumped through the aorta and into the body. With a large VSD, oxygen rich blood moves from the left ventricle back into the right ventricle (blue blood). Remember, this blood goes into the lungs and is problematic because, blood going into the lungs that is already loaded with oxygen causes pulmonary (lung) hypertension (increased pressure). (1) When this happens, the child may have labored breathing, difficulty feeding and grow poorly. The doctor explained that 40 percent of small VSDs close on their own, but Joshua's was significantly larger so it wasn't expected to close completely. The doctor explained that over time, the heart would grow and the hole would become less problematic. The cardiologist asked to see Joshua every other month to check his growth, his lungs and his blood oxygen levels.

LAUGHTER PRINCIPLE #3
Ask yourself: "What do I choose to Believe?"

During times of crisis, it is important to resist the urge to say, "Why me?" Hold onto the promise, hold onto your desires and hold onto your faith.

When people have a desire and current circumstances seem to indicate that the desire will not occur, people tend to focus on what they do not like, or the current situation, rather than focusing and waiting with that 'sweet anticipation' for the desire to culminate. This is a huge mistake. If we participate in creating our reality, then every thought we have either draws us closer or further away from our dreams and desires. Unfortunately, people tend to relish in complaining and talking about what they do not like. I promise you, doing this will guarantee that you will not see your heart's desires.

We saw the cardiologist in Richmond every other month for a little more than a year. Then something wonderful happened. The day I took Josh to the cardiologist in December 1990 was like any other day. I had stopped working when I had Josh to become a stay-at-home mother. I'd begun to investigate health issues, specifically the rise in autoimmune disease and cancer. I had just begun my quest, but the most important priority was my son's health. Through his first 13 months, he had experienced repeated upper respiratory infections and of course, we visited the cardiologist regularly.

That December, Josh was scheduled for his regular appointment. At that time, my daughter went to preschool three times a week so we scheduled our cardiologist appointments around her preschool. It was a 45 minute drive to the cardiologist's office. Josh hated to ride in cars, but for some reason, he seemed a little different that day. He was very calm and didn't cry at all in the car. I remember looking back at him in the rearview mirror and he looked at me so peacefully, so serene.

I recall the doctor always had to sedate Josh so he would be calm during the examination. This day, however, either Josh wasn't sedated or the sedation wasn't effective. We waited for him to quiet down, but I had to interrupt and say we needed to get started because I had to get back home to pick up my daughter. The cardiologist walked in and placed the scope on Josh's chest. Well, it was the shortest visit ever. The doctor looked at the monitor and viewed the ultrasound image of Josh's heart. He looked at Josh's chart, then back at the screen; then he looked at me in amazement. He put the scope down, shook his head and said, "Josh's heart is healed. The hole that was there last time is simply gone."

The doctor became quiet, and then he said, "You should be very thankful. There are some things I simply cannot explain. I'll write a letter to your pediatrician; you don't need to see me again." I wish you could have seen his face!

Wow. What a ride home. I didn't have a cell phone then, so the only ones who could share my rejoicing, were Josh, and most important of all, God. I was renewed that day. We had cleared a major hurdle. I was determined I was going to find answers to why I had an autoimmune disease and why we have seen such an increase in ADHD, autism and more.

I was convinced if I did not have Graves' disease, if I hadn't been prescribed the medication, my son wouldn't have had a heart defect. I'll never know for sure, but I was determined to at least know why.

The moral of the story is that I received a promise that day in March 1989, seven months before my child was born. I received a promise and I *chose* to believe it. What do *you* choose to believe? Every one of you has a dream, a vision, a thought, good or bad. What do you *choose* to believe? Remember to 'guard your thoughts, for they create your reality!' The evidence of my miracle wasn't realized until 13 months after Josh was born, or 20 months after the promise was given, 20 months after I *chose* to accept that promise. Even then, Josh was still plagued with illness, but I continued to believe he would be whole.

What do many of you do with a vision, thought or idea if you don't see it materialize immediately? You lose faith and push it away. I ask my children, "If you were in heaven and you wanted to ride a horse, what would you do?" They answer, "I would say, 'I want to ride a horse' and immediately, I would be on the horse." Then I ask them, "What if I told you that this is exactly how it works down here on earth? The only difference is that here on earth we are in our human bodies and the results of our thoughts and wishes are slowed down. They're not immediate, but the results are exactly the same; our experiences are the result of our thoughts!"

After a rough start, I have two children who are whole. I have a son who is not on medication, an athletic, straight A student. My children do not take any prescription medication. I've watched their personalities develop. I have been blessed. So who am I?

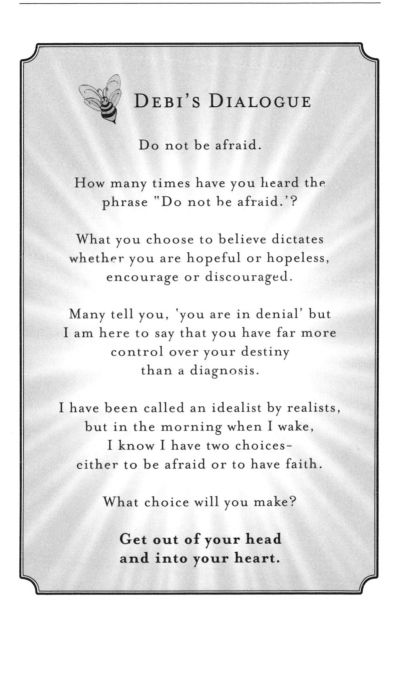

DEBI'S DIALOGUE

Do not be afraid.

How many times have you heard the
phrase "Do not be afraid.'?

What you choose to believe dictates
whether you are hopeful or hopeless,
encourage or discouraged.

Many tell you, 'you are in denial' but
I am here to say that you have far more
control over your destiny
than a diagnosis.

I have been called an idealist by realists,
but in the morning when I wake,
I know I have two choices-
either to be afraid or to have faith.

What choice will you make?

**Get out of your head
and into your heart.**

The Discovery

"A discovery is said to be an accident meeting a prepared mind."

~ ALBERT SZENT-GYORGYI

LONGEVITY PRINCIPLE #5
There is a profound relationship between wellness and absorption.

Who am I? I'm not a doctor, but I have become a great observer by asking questions and listening. The key to finding an answer is to know it has already been given. The answer is before you.

Accelerating the process comes with patience, watching and listening for opportunities and eager anticipation for the day the answer reveals itself. I was driven to continue searching because I was told I had a serious autoimmune disease and given a medication that unfortunately, was later not recommended for pregnant women. I am a person who, two months later, became pregnant with my second child, and two months after that, was told to abort that child. I am a person who gave birth to a child with a significant heart defect. Although Josh's heart was healed, from 13 months to seven years, he had frequent visits to the doctor for upper respiratory infections, croup, ear infections and more.

LAUGHTER PRINCIPLE #4
If you ask, It will be given. A gift often comes when you least expect it. Be patient and do not doubt.

By the time Josh was six years old, he had already been diagnosed with respiratory airway disease, ADHD, eczema and lazy eye. These are not life threatening conditions, but they do affect quality of life. For my son's conditions, all I had to do was give him steroids for asthma, apply steroid cream for his eczema and give him dexamphetamine for ADHD. The doctors told me that Josh's lazy eye could not be corrected because that part of his brain had already developed. So he wore glasses for his lazy eye. Compared to Josh's heart, these were minor inconveniences. I have celebrated our small victories; I was so grateful that Josh's heart had healed. However, I did not want my children living a life on prescription medications.

QUESTIONING AUTHORITY

I had several experiences that caused me to question the wisdom and authority of doctors. When Josh was 18 months old, he went in for his Tuberculosis (TB) skin test. The nurse will poke an instrument with several small needles into the skin. If the child has TB, the spot will become red and elevated like a mosquito bite. When I came back for the results of Josh's TB test, the doctor said it was positive! There was a red spot on Joshua's arm. I was shocked. I had quit work when Josh was born and he was not exposed to anyone other than my family and whatever exposure he would have when we were out and about. The doctor prescribed my baby medication that would require regular liver and kidney tests. I was very concerned about the side effects of such a powerful medication and I highly doubted the results and opinion of the doctor. I look back and wonder why at such a young age, I would dare to question the doctors? I did because on every level I was holding onto the promise I had received, that I would have a healthy baby boy. So, I found the Physicians' Desk Reference (PDR) and looked up the drug that was prescribed. I read about the side effects and complications, namely that the drug would cause impending arthritis as an adult. I went to our State Health Department and demanded a more accurate test, an injection under the skin. I did this because if Joshua had a TB diagnosis in his medical charts, it would be difficult if not impossible for him to attend regular school without treatment. Three days later I went back to the Health Department and watched as a litany of medical professionals came in, closed their eyes and felt Josh's arm. The spot was red and that triggered the diagnosis. But upon my research, I found that the skin must be red AND have induration of the skin, or a welt. There was no welt. Josh is a redhead, he has very fair skin. He also was born with inadequate inoculation from me. He was already hypersensitive to his environment. If I fed him spaghetti, his skin would turn red around his mouth for hours. If I put a band aid on his arm, once removed, you would see two bright red spots from the adhesive for days. I was sure that he did not have TB. Finally, the Health Department confirmed that he did not have TB and wrote me a letter so he could attend school.

What would you have done? Would you run to the drugstore and give your child a drug that would result in arthritis as an adult, or kidney and liver problems as a child? Many people simply act without questioning or listening to that 'still, small voice inside'. Wake Up! You know you and you know your children better than anyone. It is time to begin to pay attention.

THE PIRATE PATCH

Remember, when times are difficult, look back and remember what you have to be thankful for. Thinking about other 'misdiagnoses'- when I was told Josh had lazy eye, I did not believe it was too late to fix it, so I bought two pirate patches. I put the patch on Josh's good eye (he wouldn't do it unless I did as well, hence the two patches!) and had him wear the patch one or two hours a day for about four months. Maybe I am the one who is crazy, but Josh does not have lazy eye today! If that could happen, what else was I told that was invalid? Celebrate your small miracles! I am no one special. I chose to believe. I *chose* to believe that I would have a healthy and happy child. What do you *choose* to believe?

LAUGHTER PRINCIPLE #5
Celebrate small miracles!

Have you ever tried to look at a star? Do you notice that sometimes when you stare directly at a star, you do not see it, but when you look away, you're able to see it? Of course, the real reason is there are no reflective rods and cones at the very center of your retina where the optic nerve lies, so if you look a little off center, you can see that elusive star. Similarly, if you desperately want something, by *relaxing* into it, almost distracting yourself while you are waiting, remaining calm, happy and enthusiastically expectant, you accelerate the time it takes to receive your promise. Instead, many people focus on their problem and anxiously await the solution. This is like staring at the star, often, you can't find the answer. Relax, know the answer is coming, and enjoy you in the meantime.

How I Searched For Answers

From 1989 through 1997, corporate America moved us nine times. During that time, I was a student at Virginia Tech, Virginia Commonwealth University and Portland State University. I was a professor at Portland Community College and provided continuing education credits for the American Council on Exercise. When Josh was old enough to attend preschool and Morgan was in elementary school, I spent that time in the medical library studying the National Institute of Health's Medline and articles from the *New England Journal of Medicine.* I began my journey with a series of questions. For example, I plugged "Graves' Disease" into the computer and read every article I could. I remember the first that said, "Physicians will recommend supplementation under few conditions; burn victims and patients with Graves' Disease, due to the elevated metabolism." I was shocked. No one had told me to supplement!

LONGEVITY PRINCIPLE #6
Your current circumstances do not need
to dictate your reality or your future.

I cross referenced "supplementation" and
"Graves" disease," and I read every article I could.
For example: "Typical deficiency is vitamin A
with Graves' disease patients." I cross-referenced
"deficiency and vitamin A" and I found, "Those
deficient in vitamin A typically have low stomach
acid levels." Then I cross-referenced "low stomach
acid levels" and so on and so on. I remember an
article about cervical dysplasia that stated cells of
the cervix that are precancerous are deficient in
certain antioxidants such as carotenoids, vitamin
E and folic acid. In a related article, I found that
certain birth control pills can inhibit absorption
of—guess what, the same nutrients that are lacking
in cervical dysplasia cells. Of course, I am not
saying, "Don't take birth control pills," but I
would love to see a caveat that states, "You may

want to supplement with folic acid, vitamin E and carotenoids while taking this prescription." Now, I am seeing suggestions for a mandate that all young girls receive the human papilloma virus (HPV) vaccine to prevent cervical cancer. What if these girls needed to increase certain nutritional supplements? How long will the HPV vaccine last? What effects will another vaccine have on our health? Twenty years ago, autism was 1 in 10,000 yet today, autism is reported to be 1 in 150 children. Vaccinations have increased three fold in children since 1988. Is there a link? A great deal of controversy revolves around this issue. A preservative in vaccinations called Thimerosal depletes a precious antioxidant in our body called Glutathione. Glutathione is additionally depleted by a poorly developed intestinal area creating an immature GALT which creates a hyperactive immune system. Such a rapid decline in our health, or the health of our planet for that matter, is rarely created by one event but by a series of events.

Thus my journey began, always questioning if and why we see an increase in autoimmune disease and where it comes from. In the 1980s, the Baby

Boomers started demanding information because they wanted to feel better and they didn't want to get old! From that, an interest in prevention and nutrition picked up and we began to learn "You are what you eat!" There were public service commercials in the 80s meant to educate Americans. You may recall the "Schoolhouse Rock" cartoon, "I'm Just a Bill," which taught us how a bill becomes a law. Well, other commercials taught us about food and the food pyramid. One commercial showed a boy eating French fries and ultimately, he became a walking bag of French fries. "We are what we eat!" Over the past 20 years, we have received so much information from "Don't eat fat," to "Eat fat; fats are good," to "Don't eat carbs," to "Eat carbs, but only the good ones." During all this time, we have witnessed a rise in cancer, autoimmune diseases, attention deficit disorder, depression, allergies and more.

We've spent the past 20 years worrying about what's on our plate; but still haven't really discussed what happens once what we eat enters the body. What's going on inside?

LONGEVITY PRINCIPLE #7
If you don't have optimal health, then you are not effectively absorbing, assimilating and utilizing your nutrition.

BEES, FISH AND HUMANS LONG-TERM

The Bees are dying.

By the way, have you heard that the bees are dying? Rumor says that Albert Einstein said that if the bees were to die, mankind would have only four years left. No bees, no pollination, no plants, no food, no us. A 2001 to 2004 research project at the University of Jena studied the effects of pollen from a genetically modified corn called "GMO-BT corn" on bees. GMO stands for genetically modified organism. The GMO-BT corn has been genetically modified to have a *Bacterial Toxin* (BT) that is poisonous to insects. According to the study, "BT corn is created when a gene from a soil bacterium is inserted into corn and then enables the plant to produce its own pesticide."

The study showed that genetically modified corn alone did not harm bees; however, when these same bees were introduced to a common parasite, the parasite was able to enter the bee's body, causing a significant decline in the bee populations. (1)

The bee's intestinal area has been so damaged or altered by GMO corn that its intestinal wall has become weakened enough to allow a parasite that has existed for a millions of years to penetrate its body. States growing the most GMO-BT corn are among those suffering the greatest loss to their bee populations. Right now, 32 percent of all U.S. corn is genetically modified. Even the bee's health is affected by the health of its intestinal area!

Don't be fooled by reports that show the greatest loss of bees in Germany, where there is much less GMO-BT corn grown. Although the corn does not have a genetically inserted bacterial toxin, Germany uses an abundance of pesticides which have the same effect. The chemicals alter the intestinal area of the bee. The parasite has always been around, but now the parasite can invade the bee's intestinal area. Why? The first bees were found in fossils more than 35 million years old.

For the past 35 million years, this parasite would kill the weaker bees and natural selection would allow the stronger bees to survive until today. Unfortunately, our introduction of pesticides or poisons onto crops is affecting the bee, making even the strong now susceptible to the parasite. Chemicals are affecting our intestinal ecology which is damaging the microbe population present in humans, bees, even the ocean or simply everywhere. Microbes are present in all life forms; in fact, microbes may be the simplest life form and the health of microbes in our bodies or even a bee's body affects our overall health. We must return the balance or none of us will be here much longer.

FISH AND REPRODUCTION

Research is showing us repeatedly that human chemical intervention is harming our planet. That intervention may backfire with the drop in our bee population and now intervention in the reproduction of fish. No bees, no fish, no food. Farm raised fish, or fish hatcheries are fast becoming a hot commodity as predictions loom regarding the depletion of wild fish populations in the oceans. Farm raised fish are kept in pens and fed food and given medications. Natural selection is eliminated and hormone pellets are given to encourage reproduction. Fish raised in captivity have far more diseases than fish that are raised in the wild and severe changes in the fish environment alter not only genetics but also fishes' microbial population. The changes reduce reproductive abilities and increase disease. What is worse is that farm raised fish often escape and then breed with wild fish. An article in the June 13, 2009 issue of Science daily reported that a fish born in the wild to two hatchery fish had 37% the reproductive fitness of wild fish. A fish born in the wild where one parent was from a hatchery had 87% the reproductive fitness. We hatch farm raised fish to increase the numbers then introduce them into the wild to 'repopulate' the oceans, only to later discover that the new fish can't have babies!

Again and again we continue with harmful behaviors and mask the problem looking for solutions that are never addressing the root issue. We have raped the seas due to overly aggressive fishing and now that many species are near extinction, hatcheries are developed as a recovery effort by conservationists.

We move into urban environments with greater density of population, limited access to fresh fruits and vegetables, greater pollution and stress and disease increases and we treat with medications rather than addressing hygiene and overpopulation issues. We litter the grocery store shelves with cookies, sodas, sugar cereals, hydrogenated fats, irradiated produce and TV dinners. We litter the airwaves with commercials encouraging kids to ask their parents for junk foods and childhood obesity has soared. We remove physical education from schools and add hot dogs, French fires and chicken nuggets and have hyperactive children that we treat with a drug. We then yell for Universal Health care. What if we took the money budgeted for health care and created wellness clinics that included teaching meal planning, *affordable healthy foods,* exercise classes including childcare and rewarded participants with lowered or free health care costs? What would happen if a ten year plan encouraged citizens to not only adopt healthy lifestyles but helped them to do so and in the end rewarded them with affordable health care. During this time, free catastrophic health care would be offered to all. Can you imagine the uproar if in ten years people were penalized for smoking, or living on donuts, or for a waist size that was bigger than their hips? Is this fair? Government should not dictate how many donuts one eats, however, it would be prudent to reward individuals who actively seek a wellness program and work on improving their blood sugar, blood lipids and blood pressure through clinically proven lifestyle adaptations. This can only happen if healthy foods and wellness programs were available to all equally. Maybe this is where the money should be spent?

Obtaining a healthy lifestyle is difficult for some who live in areas without safe foot or bike paths, areas where healthy food choices are absent or the cost of personal trainers or gym memberships is prohibitive. What we do instead is ignore policy that may improve wellness applications and instead attract you to free health care and reduced costs for prescription drugs. No one talks about the elephant in the room. The government is not helping anyone get well; it is simply perpetuating sickness and offering to give it to you for free! Is that what you really want?

What would happen if city planning included

local farming sections that provided fresh produce, sliding scale child care programs or free community centers with tax rewards for those attending healthy, lifestyle classes? Urban sprawl was born out of the industrial revolution however; we have now entered the information age and no longer need to live in overcrowded environments. The age of the internet, twitter, facebook, or video phones will allow people to live more comfortably in all parts of the country that are more community oriented.

It is all about the control of money. We eagerly watch 'Deadliest Catch' without even wondering what will happen when there are no crabs left. We the people have to 'vote with our dollar' by not watching 'Deadliest Catch', by not buying farm raised fish, by protesting against genetically modified foods and so on. When we use our dollar as a mouthpiece, we may alter the course of capitalism in our country. When there is no demand, there will be no supply. We either do it now while we have time as a planet to recover, or we wait while the rich get richer and the poor get poorer and sicker. If we wait, some will prosper but many will suffer. In the end however, we will all find ourselves in the same situation. The current capitalistic behavior reminds me of a rogue teenager who runs around participating in dangerous behaviors with no contemplation of the consequences of their actions and the effects on their future. Once the bees and fish are gone, what's one to buy with their money? We will all be the same... hungry.

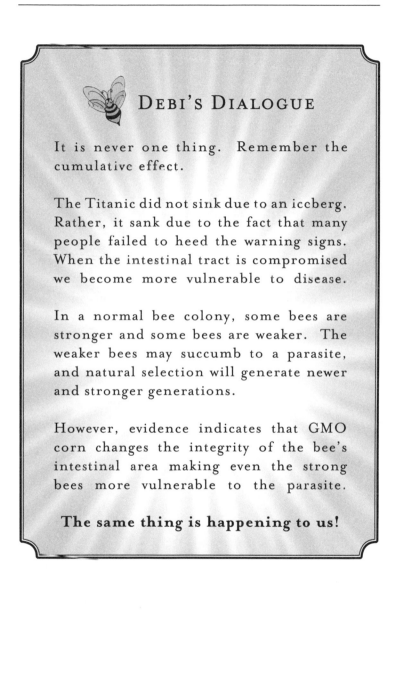

DEBI'S DIALOGUE

It is never one thing. Remember the cumulative effect.

The Titanic did not sink due to an iceberg. Rather, it sank due to the fact that many people failed to heed the warning signs. When the intestinal tract is compromised we become more vulnerable to disease.

In a normal bee colony, some bees are stronger and some bees are weaker. The weaker bees may succumb to a parasite, and natural selection will generate newer and stronger generations.

However, evidence indicates that GMO corn changes the integrity of the bee's intestinal area making even the strong bees more vulnerable to the parasite.

The same thing is happening to us!

CHAPTER

6

First Life

"The more original a discovery, the more obvious it seems afterwards."

~ ARTHUR KOESTLER

UNDERSTANDING GUT-ASSOCIATED LYMPHOID TISSUE (GALT)

Most people think the immune system consists only of lymph nodes and that swollen lymph nodes indicate an infection. In reality, lymph nodes are simply a part of the entire lymphatic system which itself is part of the immune system. The lymphatic system is much like the interrelated flow of water on our planet. As streams flow into rivers and rivers flow into the ocean, so the lymphatic system runs throughout the entire body. The entire lymphatic system is connected and an imbalance originating in one part of the system may show up in another area.   For instance, what if an imbalance that originates in the intestinal area manifests itself as asthma? We treat the asthma, but it never goes away so we manage the asthma.   Imagine treating the original source of the imbalance. Since the entire lymphatic system is connected, it makes sense that addressing the largest part of the immune system would support all other areas.

A 2004 Tufts research study (1) showed that because of these connections, the health of the GALT may directly affect the overall immune system because the lymphoid areas are related much like bodies of water on our planet are interconnected. If the GALT is affected negatively, the overall immune system is also affected negatively. If a stream is polluted, the pollution will reach the river and ultimately, the ocean. If one part of the lymphatic area is "polluted", it will affect other parts of the body.

Peter Anton, MD, and researchers at the David Geffen School of Medicine at the University of California, Los Angeles (UCLA) have recently published evidence that HIV is a disease of the Gut Associated Lymphatic Tissue. This was only published in December of 2007. In subsequent books, I hope to bring to you more research about the health of the gut and our immune system. It is exciting that research is now showing this profound relationship. Peter Anton describes the scope of the GALT as compared to the immune system.

When you take all of the lymph nodes in the body and the immune cells in the liver and spleen, and lay them out flat, it's about the size of a door. And when you lay out all of the immune cells in the intestine, various people have calculated it to be the size of a tennis court, or more probably the size of a football field. It is a descriptive metaphor that people can grasp. The amount of immune cells that are in the gut is absolutely overwhelming when compared to the rest of the body. (2)

The lymphatic system is part of the Mucosal-Associated Lymphoid Tissue, or MALT. The MALT is comprised of Lymphatic tissue and is in many parts of the body including the lungs or bronchial tubes, called the bronchial associated lymphatic tissue or BALT, and the skin, called the skin associated lymphatic tissue or SALT. MALT is also found in the intestines, or gut, and is appropriately called the gut associated lymphatic tissue or GALT. The GALT makes up 70 percent of the lymphatic system. When there is an imbalance in the GALT, which makes up a major portion of the lymphatic tissue, it is common to see an imbalance for instance in the bronchial tissue or lungs, and asthma may be the result. What if asthma were related to an imbalance in the intestinal area? Could it be that an imbalance in the GALT further pollutes the skin associated lymphatic tissue, and a consequence is eczema? Remember, the lymphatic system is interrelated. The development of the gut dramatically affects the development of other lymphatic tissue.

The intestines are related to the GALT. Therefore, the health and balance of the intestines affect the health of the GALT; this affects your health and the immune system. This is why I say there is a profound relationship between overall wellness and the ability to digest, absorb and assimilate nutrition. Anyone who is not healthy can assume the intestinal area is not healthy either. The gut trains the immune system. The intestinal area is part of your gastrointestinal tract (GI) tract. The

GI tract begins in the mouth and moves through the esophagus, stomach, small intestines and large intestines, where the colon resides. There are bacteria in all parts of the GI tract. Most bacteria, however, reside in the large intestines. In fact, 30 to 50 percent of feces are bacteria. There are more than 500 different kinds of bacteria in an adult GI tract, and the relationship and mix of these bacteria represent your bacterial "ecology." Other words for these bacteria are flora and microflora. As a population, we have thought very little about the ecology of our GI tract. We figure we eat and that's the end of the story; our bodies will do the rest. Unfortunately, three generations of significant changes in our diet and environment have dramatically altered our bacterial ecology so we now see a generation that is predicted not to live as long as its parents' generation. This is a TRAGEDY.

I hope you read and reread this book to better understand that the status of your health directly impacts the health of the next generation.

Humans receive an initial inoculation of bacteria from their mothers during the birthing process that is further developed early in life by the quality of food and supplementation as well as exposure to the environment. The quality of a mother's intestinal inoculation is passed on to the next generation. Many medical breakthroughs have allowed us to win many health battles, but we are still at war. Today, we have birthed a new generation, Generation Rx. I believe there is hope to restore our current broken intestinal ecology before the next generation. We have seen the baby boom generation, Generation X, Generation Rx, and we must prepare for our future - 'Generation Next'.

MATERNAL INOCULATION

A mother's intestinal bacteria are similar to what is found in her birth canal. So when a mother gives birth, the baby swallows vaginal fluid, making the bacteria in mother's birth canal the first "inoculation" of bacteria the baby receives. If Mom's intestinal bacteria are out of balance, then baby will begin life out of balance. When a baby is born, its intestinal area is very immature. It is sterile, which means there are no bacteria in it. Upon birth, the baby switches from amniotic fluid in its GI tract to Mom's bacteria, which are bacteria from Mom's body, the environment and any element introduced via feeding; all participate in establishing the gut ecology of bacteria. Next to the sterile intestinal area is the GALT, young and immature, waiting for its "education" from the intestinal area.

Our intestinal area is exposed to more bacteria and viruses from food in one day than the immune system will see in a lifetime. Imagine how much enters the body through food eaten—fungus, molds, viruses, bacteria, chemicals, preservatives and more. To some degree, the body knew this would happen. Foods we eat, drinks we swallow, fluid from a kiss and so on, introduce a tremendous amount of pathogens (harmful proteins) to our body. The intestinal area was designed to protect these foreign proteins from entering our blood; so our immune system is not triggered and called to action. The purpose of the GALT is to desensitize the body to invading organisms. When the intestinal area is teeming with good bacteria—or probiotics—the GALT responds normally, not hyperactively. In Chapter 2, I described antigens and antibodies. An antibody is created when the body sees a foreign invader, a foreign protein or a virus, bacteria or other pathogen. When the protein is seen as foreign, it becomes an *antigen* and will be attacked by the *antibody* that is assigned to attack it. Why would this happen and where do these foreign proteins come from?

GALT AND THE IMMUNE SYSTEM

When the intestinal area is fully developed, the GALT responds normally. The intestinal area is initially inoculated with beneficial bacteria from the mother, but it must be further developed. If you throw seed down on the ground but you never till the soil or water the seed, it will not grow. The beneficial bacteria the baby is exposed to at birth must also be developed. Oligosaccharides found in mother's milk contain special properties that act like fertilizer for these beneficial bacteria. Luckily for us, certain supplements called fructooligosaccharides (FOS) act like the oligosaccharides in a mother's milk. These special sugars have no nutritive value, but they are immensely beneficial and are called prebiotics. They are fuel for probiotics or good bacteria. I will talk more about prebiotics in Chapter 12.

When the intestinal area is properly inoculated

and developed, special antibodies in the gut, called sIgA are abundant. sIgA are a special kind of antibody. I will refer to them as IgA. As I mentioned earlier, antibodies never forget so every time they see an antigen, they will attack, even if the attack is a mistake and the antibody is attacking the body tissue. IgA in the gut are antibodies that basically attack "one time only" or better yet, make the foreign protein "invisible" to the immune system. I liken the IgA antibodies to the Klingons in the old Star Trek episodes. The Klingon's ships had a cloaking devise that would hide their ships and render them invisible. IgA antibodies are similar. They will identify, degrade and destroy foreign proteins found in the gut before the GALT or immune system ever sees them thereby lessening the chance of autoimmune disease. Remember, the intestinal area is constantly exposed to pathogens such as viruses, bacteria, fungus and more on a daily basis from the food we eat. It is very important that the proteins from these pathogens are not "seen" by our GALT. If they are, then the lymphatic system will create an antibody to attack. There is a direct relationship between gut beneficial bacteria (probiotics) and gut IgA. The more beneficial bacteria in the gut, the more special IgA antibodies. The IgA do two main things: they destroy the pathogen and they keep the pathogens invisible to the immune system reducing our chances of autoimmune disease.

This brilliant design in the normal gut keeps the immune system from being "hyperactive." A healthy intestinal area creates a healthy GALT, which *desensitizes* the immune system to its environment rather than the hyperactive immune system seen today in people with allergies, eczema, asthma, and autoimmune diseases because an underdeveloped intestinal area creates an immature GALT and thus, a hyperactive immune system. Why? Because without good bacteria and gut IgA, there are fewer special antibodies called IgA to destroy foreign proteins before they are seen by the immune system. When the intestinal area and GALT are underdeveloped, the immune system "sees" a great deal more foreign proteins from bacteria and viruses. The likelihood of creating an antibody that accidentally attacks proteins that look like us is greatly increased. This was never intended to happen with a mature GALT. A mature GALT is better able to block food proteins, viruses and other bacteria from entering the body, thereby minimizing an overactive immune system. In fact, new evidence shows that the bacteria of the gut can calm a hyper or overactive immune system, which is encouraging for those with asthma, eczema, multiple sclerosis, rheumatoid arthritis and more because there may be options other than just drugs.

PROBIOTICS AND INTESTINAL PH

Probiotics come from the mother in the birthing process and are further developed during the first two years of life in feeding and exposure to the environment. Along the entire GI tract, the ecology of bacteria produces different pH levels. Each part of the GI tract is designed for a specific pH in essence to "turn on" and "turn off" enzymes as needed. Every point of the intestinal area has a different pH to activate enzymes that only work in a specific pH. If the pH level is off or wrong, then we have a big problem. Although intestinal pH is not as acidic as that of the stomach, it is very important that the pH of the intestines is slightly acidic, around 5.3. In this state, pathogens (bad bacteria) cannot grow. (3,4) Many people who have allergies, autoimmune disease, asthma and more have an intestinal area that is too alkaline

or not acidic enough. Probiotics are acid-loving
bacteria and they *produce* acids that help destroy
bad bacteria such as strep, staph, and E. coli. (5,6)
When we have an imbalance in our intestines or
a poor ecology, meaning too much bad bacteria,
then the pH in our intestines will be higher,
around 6.7. Strep, staph and E. Coli LOVE this
pH and they will thrive. Now you have the basics.
GALT will be discussed in more detail in later
chapters.

VISUAL EVIDENCE OF IMBALANCES

Assuming there is a significant relationship
between wellness and how we digest, absorb and
assimilate (how we process and use) our nutrition,
then one telltale sign of health is the health of our
feces. If you see a car driving down the road and
it is blowing black smoke, you know the engine
has a problem. Feces are a product of what we eat
and the health of our intestinal tracts. Healthy
feces comprised of beneficial bacteria will usually
be a little more than one inch in diameter, seen
one to three times per day, be well formed and
float. There is no straining upon elimination.
(7) Too much elimination (diarrhea) or too
little elimination (constipation) are a sign of an

imbalance in intestinal bacteria. Dr. Oz mentions that feces should be in an 'S' shape which is the shape of the later part of your colon and rectum. Feces that are pencil thin, or hard and in small chunks are evidence of poor ecology of bacteria in the gut. Feces that are full and well formed move along the intestinal track and widen the colon. The colon is not a smooth tube but rather has many folds and pockets. Imagine a smooth piece of aluminum foil. Now ball it up, then open it up and attempt to smooth it out. You will see many folds and wrinkles. The wall of the colon also has folds and wrinkles. Well formed feces open these wrinkles up. If feces are thin or come out in small hard pieces, it is probable that feces are being left behind in the folds of the colon. Over time, the left behind feces can become impacted, infected and lead to polyps, diverticulitis or worse.

LONGEVITY PRINCIPLE #8
Talking about our health and our immune system without including the health of the intestinal area is like arguing about what octane gas to put in the car when the engine has a head gasket leak.

So the real question becomes: *Are we really what we eat, or are we what we absorb, digest and assimilate?* People with ailments as simple as allergies, migraines, autoimmune disease, ADHD or ailments as serious as cancer may have one thing in common: A high rate of digestive dysfunction (intestinal area not operating optimally) which damages the development of the GALT and negatively affects the immune system. This leads to an immune system that doesn't function properly.

There are a host of microbes (bacteria) in your digestive tract, actually about three pounds worth! These microbes have many functions from helping you digest your nutrition to processing and producing some of your vitamins to protecting you from known harmful substances and more. The main types of microbes are:

1) **Achaea** live in extreme environments, such as in the deep ocean near boiling hot volcanic vents (there are none of these microbes in our bodies!).

2) **Bacteria** are related to archaea, and are found everywhere. When you have a bowel movement, your feces are 1/3 to 2/3 bacteria. For every cell in your body, there are ten bacteria. How can we avoid the importance of microbes? Bacteria can cause disease, but they also can produce vitamins in your intestinal area, such as vitamin B necessary for serotonin levels (low levels are indicated in depression) and vitamin K (low levels are often indicated in spider veins and bruising) or Biotin (low levels may be evident by cradle cap in babies).

3) **Viruses** are actually parasites, but cannot function unless inside a host. Viruses are the smallest microbe and some experts wonder whether they are not actually little pieces of larger cells. They have no DNA, so they seem to

be unique in and of themselves, but are they?

There are both good and bad bacteria, and trying to get rid of all of the bad is not the answer. Rather, we want a balance between the good and bad; a healthy ecology of bacteria where a mutually beneficial symbiosis between various kinds of microbes enhance and benefit one another. The microbial population of the intestinal area plays an essential role in how the Gut-Associated Lymphoid Tissue (GALT) affects the immune system. Remember: The gut trains the immune system, and it begins at birth.

The quality of these intestinal bacteria is what "programs" the GALT and plays a role in how the immune system will function. The GALT helps desensitize the immune system. However, with the huge increase in autoimmune disease and allergies, it is obvious the integrity of the GALT has been damaged; therefore, the immune system becomes sensitive to many normally non threatening invaders, including food. Additionally, toxins and undigested proteins can enter the bloodstream and contribute to illness.

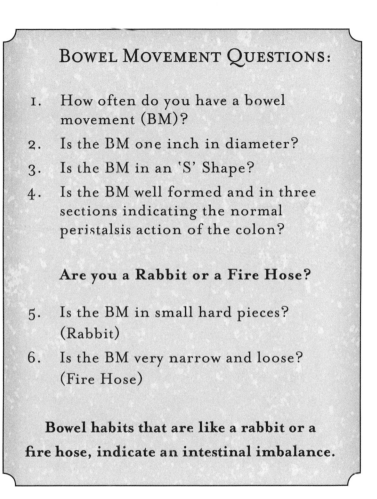

BOWEL MOVEMENT QUESTIONS:

1. How often do you have a bowel movement (BM)?
2. Is the BM one inch in diameter?
3. Is the BM in an 'S' Shape?
4. Is the BM well formed and in three sections indicating the normal peristalsis action of the colon?

Are you a Rabbit or a Fire Hose?

5. Is the BM in small hard pieces? (Rabbit)
6. Is the BM very narrow and loose? (Fire Hose)

Bowel habits that are like a rabbit or a fire hose, indicate an intestinal imbalance.

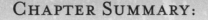

CHAPTER SUMMARY:

1. The lymph system is a major component of the immune system.
2. 70% of the lymph system is comprised of the Gut Associated Lymphoid Tissue (GALT).
3. The GALT is intimately connected with the intestinal area.
4. Some of the most important active immune cells in the intestinal area are the IgA antibodies.
5. Intestinal IgA act differently than other antibodies in that they degrade foreign proteins and destroy them before they are 'seen' by the immune system thereby avoiding a continual immune response as seen in allergy, asthma, eczema, inflammation and autoimmune disease.
6. Research shows, the more probiotics the more IgA antibodies.
7. Probiotics are enhanced by oligo-saccharides called prebiotics.
8. An imbalanced intestinal area leads to an immature GALT which leads to an overactive immune system.

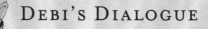

DEBI'S DIALOGUE

We were created to be well. Our bodies were created to heal themselves. If you are not well, then you are not in balance.

Balance comes from acquiring peace, harmony, clean air and water and beneficial nutrition.

Do you really think that if you were in a "Garden of Eden" with clean water and air, no stress and balanced foods, that you would get sick?

Why do you 'catch' disease? Why do you 'get' cancer? Something has happened in your body to make you susceptible. This is not complicated. Don't think that just because 'your mama' got it, that you will too. Do not be afraid.

The inoculation we receive during the first few years of life directly affects the GALT which then 'trains' the immune system. The underdeveloped GALT creates a hyperactive immune system.

The Revelation

"All truths are easy to understand once they are discovered; the point is to discover them."
~ GALILEO GALILEI

S eeing a statement on a bumper sticker was a moment of truth for me. My "Revelation" occurred in September 1996. I was on my way to the doctor for yet another round of antibiotics for my son for yet another upper respiratory condition when I found myself "zoning back in" at a red light. Does that ever happen to you? You pass your exit and you don't even remember? Well, I found myself behind an old Subaru that was held together by a hundred bumper stickers! That's when I saw it, a brand new, white bumper sticker in the midst of those faded and torn (1):

Insanity is Doing the Same Thing and Expecting a Different Result

At that moment I was born again. I was made anew; my eyes were opened. I knew it; I was insane! You may laugh, but in a way, it was quite liberating. I had spent the first six years of my son's life "doing the same thing over and over again" and expecting, hoping for healing! He was diagnosed repeatedly with ear infections. The answer—antibiotics. He was diagnosed with upper respiratory infections. The answer—antibiotics. He was diagnosed with asthma or respiratory airway disease and was prescribed steroid inhalers. He was diagnosed with eczema and was prescribed steroid ointment. He was diagnosed with ADHD and... I kept doing the same thing, over and over and over again... expecting a different result.

LAUGHTER PRINCIPLE #6
If you are stuck in a rut, maybe you need to ask new and different questions.

Rather than "Why me?" or "Why am I here?" say,
"Okay, now what do we do about it?" Forget the
blame game and get busy making a change. On that
day, I turned the car around and went home. In
the six years since Josh's heart was healed, I'd gone
back to school and studied and studied so I could
make the right choices and participate in my son's
total healing. For part of that time, I conducted
workshops for the American Council on Exercise
in the areas of health and fitness. I have to tell
you, I had the "Yeast Connection" cookbook
memorized. There were no garbage cereals or
toaster pops in my house. I made hummus and
put it in jars and told my kids it was Cheez Whiz
(It worked for a while)! My point is that I did all
the right things. I listened to the doctor. I fed
my family healthy, whole, organic food—but guess
what? We were only getting worse! Why has there
been such a rise in allergies, ADHD, depression,
autoimmune disease and cancer when many of us
are doing a lot of the right things?

"During the 1990s, there was a 700 percent
increase in the use of psycho stimulants, with the
United States consuming nearly 90 percent of
the world's supply of the drugs." (2) As of 1999,

school nurses across the U.S. delivered more medications for mental health conditions than for any other chronic health problem, and more than half were specifically for ADHD.

-Increase in Ritalin Use-
data in millions of daily dosages

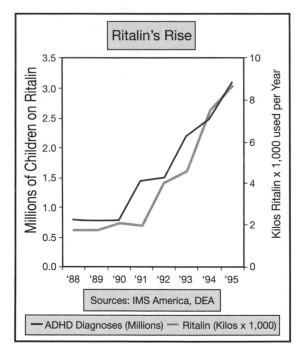

As of 2001, an estimated five to six million children in the U.S. were receiving ADHD-related drug treatment. There has been a staggering increase in these psycho-stimulating medications for our children and the prescriptions are rising.

WHERE WILL IT STOP?

ADHD, short for Attention Deficit Hyperactivity Disorder, is a condition where patients have abnormal brain wave activity; when they should be focusing, their brain waves show them daydreaming. This is an imbalance in the theta and beta brain wave activity. Beta brainwaves are active when we are alert or thinking and theta brain waves are active when we are daydreaming. Those with ADHD try to think and have an increase in the daydreaming theta brain waves. ADHD is termed a neurophysiologic condition categorized as a condition of the nervous system. Many studies have shown that removing foods that cause reactions, whether in hyperactivity or "spacing out" (theta brain wave activity), and removing artificial colors are beneficial for children with ADHD. In another study, two large groups of children with ADHD were separated and treated differently. One group got the traditional treatment of Ritalin; the second group received whole foods and nutritional supplementation. The children who received whole foods and nutritional supplementation did slightly better than those who received Ritalin. (4)

GOVERNMENT PROGRAMS AND RITALIN

What concerns me is that the increased use of Ritalin may have been stimulated by several government programs. In the 1990s, the Supplemental Security Income (SSI) program handed out cash to low income parents whose children were diagnosed with ADHD—which the government accepts as a learning disability. Moms would tell their kids to "act crazy" to receive more government money. Then in 1991, the Department of Education said schools could get hundreds of thousands of dollars in special education grant money each year for every child diagnosed with ADHD. As you can see from the chart above, ADHD diagnosis and Ritalin use was relatively flat, but after 1992, both skyrocketed. (5) Yet research shows that food and dietary choices and changes have an immense impact on these children. Worst of all, Ritalin is sold in schools as a drug by children since the effects of Ritalin for a child who doesn't have ADHD are similar to that of speed or cocaine.

So after my personal bumper sticker inspired revelation, I became an observer and kept a journal of everything that went in and out of my children and all behaviors in between. I went back to school, but became frustrated because so many of my questions weren't being answered. As I mentioned, our diet was clean. We had cut refined sugars. We ate complex carbohydrates. We took Omega 3's three times a week. Omega 3's come from fish oils and contains DHA and EPA, which are beneficial fats. Omega 3's can be supplemented or obtained from eating foods such as salmon, tuna, sardines or anchovies. Flaxseeds also contain Omega 3's; however, in forever young and vibrant, I will show that Omega 3's from fish oils have greater beneficial value. These beneficial fats are known to participate in forming the brain prenatally and in breast-feeding infants. In fact, mothers who take Omega 3's during pregnancy have infants with higher IQs. My family never drank soda or Kool-Aid. Back in 1996, I had already cut hydrogenated fats, refined flour and sugar from our diets. I was perplexed! How about you? Have you made positive food choices, but still haven't seen a significant improvement in your overall health? If so, read on.

MOTIVATION COMES FROM WITHIN

I could probably tell you in one page what I observed in how foods and our environment shaped Josh's health and all of our immune systems. But what I've found is that motivation does not come from without; it comes from within. And it comes from a deep understanding of *why*. I understand that for some, the answer was one prayer and one healing. That doesn't happen to everyone. Have you ever been to a conference or lecture and walked away totally motivated only to find the motivation dwindle in a matter of days? I have found that if I simply tell you what to do, you may comply, but soon, old habits will prevail. If however, you have a deep understanding of why, and you begin to take small and successful steps, then you are on your way to a renewed you!

I remember in 1992 as I started to see the correlation between health and wellness, I prayed to God. I did not want to be a false prophet, "If by your stripes we are healed." Then what would be the purpose of my message? I prayed and I heard, "If someone went to an altar and received a healing, and then in ignorance went back out and continued the behavior that caused his disease, and the disease came back, then what would happen to his faith? Sometimes the answer to prayer comes in the form of knowledge!"

I started a journey where I was looking for answers, so I asked questions. I found that indeed, when you ask, you will receive. Therefore, as we continue, let's acknowledge that this is a journey where we will ask and answer questions. We must also agree on the issues. Do you agree with me that we're seeing an increase in autoimmune disease? Do you agree that we are seeing a rise in cancer? Do you agree that we are seeing an increase in ADD, ADHD, depression and more?

IRRITATED INTO ACTION

My goal is not only to make you think; my goal is to prompt you into action! Have you ever wondered, "What's the missing link in all of this? Is the rise in autoimmune disease and cancer all because of genetics?" If you believe in evolution, then you can't have your cake and eat it, too. What I mean is that although it is true we evolve and adapt to our environment, this takes many generations. A generation in humans is approximately 25 years. This means we've seen three generations since the beginning of the Baby Boom generation, yet we have seen significant changes in the last three generations, or since around 1946. It's hard to blame the increase in disease on genetics alone. If genetics are solely responsible, then why didn't we see these health challenges in such high numbers three generations ago? It takes more than three generations to make such significant changes, genetically. Therefore, we must acknowledge that something more than just genetics is contributing to this change.

Genes and my Collie

We own a collie that we purchased from a well known breeder who has shown in Westminster, London. Our breeder has shown collies for 40 years and in her career, has probably bred 50 to 75 generations of collies. Remember, a generation in human terms is 25 years. A generation for a dog is as little as one year. A generation is the amount of time from infancy to normal reproductive years. Although girls today can have children at the onset of puberty, our culture has created a society where the average woman has most of her children in her late twenties to early thirties. When you go to the dog shows, you know when you see a collie bred from my breeder. Fifty generations of collies has resulted in a distinctive face and a distinctive look. However, if you had looked at her collies 39 years ago after 3 litters, you would not have seen the changes she engineered over 50 or 75 generations. It takes more than three generations to make significant genetic changes! The dramatic changes that have been witnessed in our health, since the Baby Boom generation, represents just three generations. You cannot blame the changes in our current health or the increases in cancer and autoimmune disease on genetics alone!

FOLLOW THE MONEY

The other day, I was checking out at the grocery store and the clerk asked me whether I wanted to donate a dollar to the children's leukemia fund. I asked, "Who's sponsoring this?" The clerk answered, "Pepsi-Cola." Do you think possibly, that if our children didn't drink so many sodas, that just possibly, we would not see such an increase in cancer? *Maybe, just maybe.* Or how about McDonald's? Isn't it interesting to see a donation container for the Ronald McDonald House sitting on the counter next to the cash register? Do you think, maybe, just maybe, if we didn't eat so much fast food, we wouldn't see such an increase in health challenges? Wouldn't it be wonderful if we didn't need Ronald McDonald Houses at all?

There has been a war between the traditional medical community and the alternative medical community. It is much the same war that existed between the beliefs of Louis Pasteur and the beliefs of immunologists Elie Metchnikoff and Antoine Béchamp. Pasteur's idea was that in order to eradicate disease, we must eradicate the germ. Metchnikoff, however, felt it impossible to eradicate the germ. Rather, we must alter the environment the germ lives in (the body) so the germ will not thrive. The reality is that both are correct. There is also a war between faith based groups and science about the history of man and evolution. Can they also both be right? Some preach, teach and expect for answers to prayer to fall out of the sky, to strike them with a lightning bolt! Though that can happen for some, as I mentioned, for some the answer to prayer comes in the form of knowledge and awareness.

ASKING QUESTIONS

It is time for us to ask questions. The reality is we must acknowledge the choices we as a society have made over the last 50 years, and we must acknowledge the consequences. As I began my search for answers, I was led by questions. The first question I asked myself was, "How are you?" Interestingly, I've learned that our society often responds to this question with an untruth! "How are you?" "Fine." Really? My question is, "Are you really fine?" It's all relative.

"How are you financially?" "Fine." Really? Compared to the bum on the street or compared to Bill Gates? Then the answer changes. So first let's define that word, "Fine."

Do you wake up at six or seven in the morning after you are finished sleeping, and do you feel fully rested? Do you need your morning java to wake up? Do you get on with your day and then when it gets to be about 3:00 p.m., do you need some caffeine and sugar to make it through the afternoon or are you full of energy? Do you get home at five or six in the evening and feel fantastic? Do you kiss your husband or wife, take care of the kids, make dinner and head out to the PTA meeting or business meeting feeling great? Then do you get home at 10:00 or 11:00 p.m. to finish that last load of laundry and finally drop into bed, where your head hits the pillow and you *sleep deeply*, and wake again because you are fully rested and done sleeping, ready to get on with your day? Do you laugh easily? My question is, *"How are you?"*

You see, what I've described is natural, although it may not be normal. It isn't natural to get up when you don't want to, go somewhere you don't really want to go, work with people you don't like and do something you don't really want to do. But this is your job, this is your life and this may be normal, but it certainly isn't natural! What has become normal is needing to take sleeping pills to make it through the night, needing caffeine to make it through the morning, needing sugar to make it through the afternoon, needing pain killers and antidepressants to make it through life, needing male enhancement formulas to make it through, well... and needing antacids to make it through a meal! This may have become normal, but I assure you, this is not natural!

LAUGHTER PRINCIPLE #7
Sometimes the greatest truths are
the simplest.

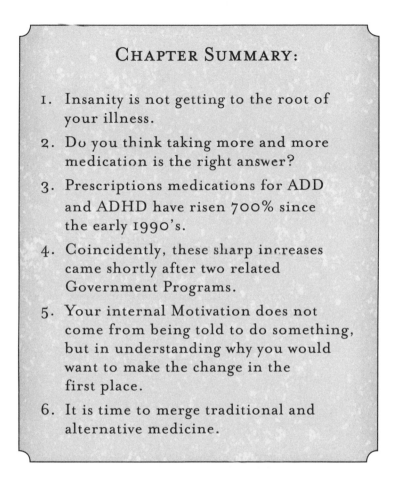

Chapter Summary:

1. Insanity is not getting to the root of your illness.

2. Do you think taking more and more medication is the right answer?

3. Prescriptions medications for ADD and ADHD have risen 700% since the early 1990's.

4. Coincidently, these sharp increases came shortly after two related Government Programs.

5. Your internal Motivation does not come from being told to do something, but in understanding why you would want to make the change in the first place.

6. It is time to merge traditional and alternative medicine.

DEBI'S DIALOGUE

Time is running short. It is time to stop pointing fingers, time to stop the blame game. Our society has become greedy as evidenced by the large number of lawsuits filed every day. If we could stop blaming and instead acknowledge the truth, then we could finally move forward and create a solution.

I saw a report today of a woman who is suing *Victoria Secret* for a rash from a bra she bought. Turns out, the bra had formaldehyde on it.

I have a 'Secret' for this lady,
-WASH THE BRA FIRST!

I promise you that politicians will not solve your problems. It is we, the people, who need to stand up and use our voice. It is time to ask 'why'? It is time we demand answers and then apply the solutions.

It is time.

CHAPTER

8

Observations

"The real voyage of discovery consists not in seeking new landscapes but in having new eyes."
~ MARCEL PROUST

When I was a little girl my father took us to see the movie *Herbie the Love Bug*. I remember being in our old, two door, red Chevy Vega with four kids in the back. I asked excitedly, "Daddy, what is a Love Bug?" and he answered, "You'll find out soon enough." I had never seen a love bug.

Well, after the movie and a ton of peanut brittle, as we drove home, I think I must have counted 186 "Love Bugs" between the theater and our home! Now, where did they come from? Did they all just instantly appear? Of course not! They were always there, but until there's awareness, you cannot see what you do not know. So let me share with you how I became aware of the relationship between wellness and absorption. After my 'bumper sticker' moment, I began studying and recording my son's every move. After about 90 days is when it happened, that was when I had a peek into what could be the source of his issues.

LAUGHTER PRINCIPLE #8
Until there is awareness, we cannot see what we do not know!

As I mentioned, I quit my job while I was pregnant with Josh, and along the way, I studied voraciously. Money was tight so I became quite creative in my endeavor to stay at home, taking on odd jobs so I could spend time with our children and study, study, study health and nutrition. I did some volunteer work with the local "Reptile Man." Mind you, this was long before Steve Irwin, the "Crocodile Hunter." The Reptile Man took his show on the road to schools, showing the kids the good snakes and the bad snakes. "Red touches black, he's a nice jack. Red touches yellow—Kill the fellow!" He ended his show with a 25 foot python the teachers held, teachers screaming and kids squealing. It was great! I was the cool mom with snakes for necklaces and I helped teach the kids.

One afternoon, we were invited to my son's school. He was almost seven years old. All the first and second graders paraded into the auditorium. My son was hard to miss with his bright red hair, his glasses and a patch of eczema on his face. I went over to greet him, and he looked up through his glasses with a dazed look on his face and slowly said hello. Now, if you have a child with ADHD, you notice that sometimes they are coming out of their skin, and sometimes they just can't focus... they're not there. Well at this moment, Josh was not present.

Since I kept a journal of everything, I went to the teacher and asked what the kids had for lunch. I had packed hummus and tabouli that day on pita bread with some dried mangos for Josh and that didn't elicit this dazed response. The teacher told me that since they had the "snake show" coming to school, the room mothers had come with a lunch that included peanut butter and a few other things. Hmm. I called a friend who is an environmental allergist and learned that peanuts are high in mold and that people with the dysfunction I am going to mention react more strongly to it. Mind you, this was just before the onset of so many peanut allergies and before we were banned from bringing homemade foods to school!

I have always been curious about the dramatic increase in peanut allergies. My cousin's daughter is deathly allergic to peanuts and everything has to be monitored. Why? I learned that an immunization will include an adjuvant, and some adjuvants are from peanut oil:

Adjuvant (ad·ju·vant) (aj´ə-vənt, ă-joo´vənt) [L. adjuvans aiding] 3. In immunology, a nonspecific stimulator of the immune response, such as BCG vaccine.

Adjuvant 65 trademark for a water-in-oil emulsion containing antigen in peanut oil with

Arlacel A and aluminum monostearate as the emulsifying agent. *Source: Dorlands Medical Dictionary*

Adjuvants were first developed in the 1920's to boost immunity and immune responses to administered antigens in vaccinations. Adjuvant 65 contains peanut oil and is added to some vaccinations to enhance our immune response. Adjuvant 65 appeared about 15 years ago. Hmmm? When did the sudden onset of deadly peanut allergies begin? Adjuvants increase shelf life of vaccinations, and reduce the number of vaccinations needed for a specific condition, since adjuvants seem to stimulate a longer immune response in our bodies. A 2001 Journal of the American Medical Association article reported that the increase in peanut allergies is due to mother's eating peanuts while pregnant or while nursing. Hmmm?? How long have mothers eaten peanuts while pregnant or nursing? For thousands of years? But now, we see an increase in peanut allergies? I am not saying, 'don't vaccinate', but could we the people demand single dose vials that do not require ingredients like Thimerosal (used as a preservative in multidose dials)? Certainly, we can question the wisdom of using peanut oil as an adjuvant.

Rapid Changes

The allergist told me to make sure Josh didn't have peanut butter for at least four days and then to have him write his name, feed him a little peanut butter, wait 15 minutes and have him write his name again. So that is what I did. I waited four days and I had him write his name:

Then I fed him one piece of toast with peanut butter on it. I waited 15 minutes and then asked him to write his name again:

Remember, I'd been told that Josh had ADHD. Now, I'm not a doctor and I had no access to a personal MRI machine for brain imaging. But, as a reasonably intelligent person, I had to ask, "If this is ADHD, why could I create the same behavior in 15 minutes by putting something into his mouth?" Why is it that two women can go into the mall and smell the fragrances and one gets a migraine and one doesn't? Why is it that when your two friends enter their thirties, one gets multiple sclerosis and the other doesn't? Why? Is it all genetic?

As I asked myself these questions, I was frustrated because we were already employing healthy eating habits and listening to the doctors, yet each year, we had a new diagnosis. What was to come next year? So at that time, I stopped studying nutrition in the traditional sense. I had studied the fat soluble vitamins, A, D, E and K and I had studied the water soluble vitamins like the B vitamins and vitamin C. I studied minerals and the sources of these nutrients. I had studied proteins, with their four calories per gram, and fats, with their nine calories per gram. Clearly, I needed to take a new approach. So I decided to look at both nutrition and medicine from a more global perspective.

Before I take you where I want to take you, let's look at where we've been and where we are. Then we'll discuss where we are going.

DEBI'S DIALOGUE

In the movie, The Matrix, Laurence Fishburne's character Morpheus gives computer programmer Thomas Anderson, played by Keanu Reeves a choice, "do you want the red pill or the blue pill?" If he takes the blue pill, he will become blissfully unaware and if he takes the red pill, he will learn that he is the master of his destiny and all is not as it seems.

The question is that simple. You can continue to believe you are not in control and continue to rely on drugs to 'fix' you, or you can decide now that you will take control of your life and begin to make decisions based on simplicity and clarity and become the Director in your own life.

**Stop fooling yourself,
take the red pill.**

Then and Now

"A disease is to be cured naturally by man's own power, and physicians help it."

~ Hippocrates

Hippocrates was a Greek physician born in 460 BC in Greece. He is known as the father of medicine and the greatest physician of his time. As a doctor, he studied the human body, but based his medical practice on observations. More importantly, he believed that the body must be treated as a whole, rather than a study of individual parts and systems. (1) He believed in the natural healing process of rest, a good diet, fresh air and cleanliness. He observed that different patients were better able to cope with specific diseases and in his day, taught that there was a relationship between our beliefs, feelings and thoughts and our health.

A car will not run without gas. Isn't it interesting, for much of our medical history, doctors have spent very little time understanding the fuel that goes into our bodies driving and sustaining us? Let's go on a journey to understand better how the study of nutrition even began and where and why we have ended up here. We cannot correct a problem unless we first recognize that the problem is there.

The Journey of Nutrition Therapy and the Resistance to Change.

1500's—Scientist and artist Leonardo da Vinci compared the process of metabolism in the body to burning a candle.

1553—Cartier made his second voyage to Newfoundland. Of his 103-man crew, 100 developed scurvy. Scurvy, a painful and deadly bleeding disorder, is an absolute absence of vitamin C. There was no knowledge of vitamin C in 1553, but the Iroquois Indians of Quebec came to Cartier's rescue. With no knowledge of vitamin C, the Iroquois offered a miraculous cure. They gave those plagued with scurvy a remedy of leaves and bark from the pine tree.

During the same era, Admiral Richard Hawkins noted that during his naval career, thousands of sailors at his command died of scurvy. Yet Hawkins made an interesting observation. He saw that oranges and lemons had been beneficial in curing this disease.

1747—Approximately 200 years later, Dr. James Lind, a British Naval physician, conducted a nutritional scientific experiment while at sea. As mentioned earlier, at the time, sailors on long sea voyages developed scurvy. Normally the only foods brought on board ships were nonperishable foods such as dried meat and breads because fresh food wouldn't last. In his experiment, Lind gave one group of sailor's sea water, the second group vinegar and the third group received limes. Those given limes were spared the devastating effects of scurvy. (1) (Well, it was actually lemons, but the Brits called them limes.)

Dr. Lind published a book in 1753 in which he stated explicitly that scurvy could be eliminated simply by supplying sailors with lime juice. Believe it or not, some say this is why the Brits came to be known as "Limies!" I wonder whether this is why those from New Zealand are known as "Kiwis".

Lind later became the head physician at the Naval Hospital at Portsmouth, England. He cited many case histories from his experience as a naval surgeon at sea. He proved that many foods, such as oranges, mustard cress and lemons, could prevent scurvy. Remember, there was no knowledge yet of vitamin C; however, food that contained enough vitamin C, most abundant in citrus fruit, tomatoes and even some green vegetables and other fruit, could prevent the dreaded scurvy of the day.

Some say Lind did not understand the magnitude of his discovery and credit was given to Sir Gilbert Blane, a Scottish physician, an advocate for improving sailors' health by urging them to heed their diet and enforce careful sanitary practices. Largely due to his advocacy, in 1795 the entire Scottish Navy began to use lime juice to prevent scurvy. And so, in 1747, Dr. James Lind performed what may have been the first controlled clinical trial and found that oranges rapidly dispersed scurvy, yet the idea was ridiculed by both British academia and the Navy. It just didn't make sense to people. I'll bet you think Dr. James Lind was a hero! In fact, he was ridiculed.

These men found a relationship between
wellness and absorption of nutrients.

Can there in fact be a profound relationship between wellness and absorption? So profound that addressing the health of the intestinal area and the body's ability to absorb should be a staple in every protocol to address health today? *Yes!*

Dr. Lind reportedly was completely frustrated that his peers found it too difficult to believe a fatal disease could be cured by simple means. Like any conflict, there are always two sides. Those sea captains who chose to listen to Dr. Lind and stock their ships with his special foods saw an elimination of scurvy at sea. Captain James Cook stocked his ships with fresh fruits. He was elected a member of the Royal Society in 1776 for his success as an explorer. Yet he was never honored for his lifesaving choices of supplying his crew with fruits and vegetables. Not until 1794, the year of Dr. Lind's death, was a British navy squadron supplied with lemon juice before a voyage. On that voyage, which lasted 23 weeks, there was not one case of scurvy. Yet another decade passed before regulations were enacted that required sailors to drink a daily ration of lemon juice to prevent scurvy. With this, scurvy disappeared from the British Navy. Why the needless loss of life?

For 251 years, sailors died—all because people refused to change, even in the face of the evidence. It is really because they did not yet embrace an awareness of facts.

THE BIRTH OF UNDERSTANDING

1770—Antoine Lavoisier, "The Father of Nutrition and Chemistry," discovered how foods are metabolized and the heat that is created through this process. This was the beginning of the understanding of a calorie and metabolism that uses food and oxygen and produces water and heat as a by-product.

Early 1800's—The four elements of foods were discovered: carbon, nitrogen, hydrogen and oxygen. Additionally, methods for measuring the amounts of these elements were developed.

1840—Justus Liebig of Germany discovered that carbohydrates were made of sugars, fats were fatty acids, and proteins were made up of amino acids.

What saddens me is that many notable scientists make

sound observations, only to be ignored or mocked by their colleagues. Oftentimes later, their observations are proven true. Dr. Igaz Semmelweiss was one such physician. In 1847, more than 18 percent of patients died in hospitals due to infectious disease contracted in the hospitals. Dr. Semmelweiss surmised the reason could be because physicians did not wash their hands between patients. Procedures were established where doctors washed their hands between visits and sterilized their hands even further with chloride lime solution after autopsies. Additionally, doctors changed into clean lab coats before seeing patients. As a result, death rates declined from 18.27 percent to less than one percent. (2)

It is hard to believe, but Semmelweis was fired for his unorthodox views. At a new hospital, Semmelweis instilled the same procedures and infectious death rates declined, while they increased again at the hospital from where he had been fired.

"Simplify, simplify."
~ HENRY DAVID THOREAU

Why couldn't people believe that disease could be cured by something so simple? Ultimately, Semmelweis was ridiculed and became so ashamed he was involuntarily committed to an insane asylum, where he died in 1865.

1897—Scientists continued to find relationships between disease and diet. Christiaan Eijkman was a Dutchman who worked with natives in Java. Some of the natives developed beriberi, which causes heart problems and neurological problems such as paralysis. Eijkman noted that chickens also developed beriberi when they were fed white rice. When the chickens ate brown rice, they were healthy. So Eijkman gave the natives brown rice and they were cured.

1912—Dr. Casmir Funk, a Polish biochemist, was the first to coin the term "vitamins" as vital factors in the diet. He wrote about these unidentified substances present in food, which could prevent the diseases of scurvy, beriberi and pellagra (a disease caused by a deficiency of niacin, vitamin B-3).

The term "vitamin" is derived from the words *vital* and *amine,* because vitamins are required for life and they were originally thought to be amines—compounds derived from ammonia. In 1929 (before the discovery of Vitamin B1), Christiaan Eijkman and Sir Frederick Gowland Hopkins received a joint

Nobel prize for identifying that the husk of brown rice had components that prevented beriberi. Later it was learned that vitamin B1 (thiamin) was the special component in the husk. These were exciting times because some diseases were being cured by food.

This was the beginning of an exciting journey!

Why did these amazing observations about the relationship between citrus fruits and scurvy go unheralded? We see one "Love Bug," we see two "Love Bugs," and we don't know about "Love Bugs." They go unnoticed. They were there all along, but we don't "see" them. Then, we become aware... and all of a sudden we see "Love Bugs" everywhere! Why does it take so long? Because people resist change!

Remember, in 1911, there were no "Love Bugs"—no vitamins—but awareness occurred for the next 40 years. Medical experts were excited by this discovery and research scientists began to isolate and identify these vital life forces. All across the world, new vitamin and preventative health approaches were heralded.

Discovery of Vitamins:

1912	Vitamin A	1934	Vitamin B-6
1922	Vitamin D	1935	Vitamin K
1922	Vitamin E	1937	Niacin
1926	Vitamin B-2	1938	Pantothenic Acid
1933	Folic Acid	1948	Vitamin B-12

(Rosenfeld, 1997)

1912—E.V. McCollum, while working for the U.S. Department of Agriculture at the University of Wisconsin, developed an approach that opened the way to the widespread discovery of nutrients. He decided to work with rats rather than large farm animals. Using this procedure, he discovered the first fat soluble vitamin, vitamin A. He found rats that were fed butter were healthier than those fed lard, as butter contains more vitamin A. The discovery that butter was healthier than lard came one year after Crisco was introduced into the average American's household kitchen, replacing butter. Yet according to the American Heart Organization's history of hydrogenated fats, this research was only proved in the 1990's, a full 80 years later! This is simply not true. Could it be that we do not know many things because we are not told? As I said in the introduction of this book, I became agitated as a late teen after I spent countless hours spray starching my own shirt only to find I could never get the same look as those with shirts professionally starched. I do not like the fact that there is much valuable information out there, yet we as consumers are completely unaware. Why is this so?

During the first half of the last century, discovery of these vitamins helped eliminate disease—scurvy, beriberi, pellagra, just to name a few—caused by lack of certain nutrients. These diseases were as commonplace then as heart disease, cancer, Alzheimer's, fibromyalgia and chronic fatigue are today.

But then around 1948, after so many exciting discoveries and clinical discussions, medicine seemed to change course. Medicine's focus shifted from prevention and nutrition to medical techniques and pharmaceuticals.

Why did we stop here when...

- 1930's—William Rose discovered the essential amino-acids, the building blocks of protein.
- 1930's Albert Szent-Gyorgl, Ph.D. isolated vitamin C?

- In 1934, doctors discovered that heart valves and muscles depended on vitamin C.
- In 1936, doctors found that vitamin C could combat polio and provide resistance to diphtheria.
- In 1936, doctors realized that vitamin C influenced glucose tolerance.
- 1937, doctors found that vitamin C and the amino acid glutathione could inactivate viruses.
- In 1938, scientists discovered that vitamin C could alleviate allergy like sensitivities.
- In the 1940s water soluble vitamin B was discovered.
- In the 1940s, Russell Marker perfected a method for synthesizing the female hormone progesteron from a component of wild yams called diosgenin.

Famous Quotes:

• "In the 1950s the Schute Brothers... said Vitamin E worked against heart disease and cerebrovascular disease as well as prevented spontaneous abortion in first trimester. They were greeted with laughter. Later the Harvard School of Public Health showed that just 100 units of Vitamin E per day decreased the death rate from cardiovascular disease by 40 percent. How many Americans would have been saved in the intervening 35 years had Harvard taken a responsible position and said: 'we are skeptical of these claims, but let's look at them?' But they wouldn't do that. It didn't fit their paradigm. So Vitamin E was totally destroyed by the establishment. Think of the cost of those decisions.
~ Linus Pauling, 1996

• "In one case where complete remission was achieved in myelogenous leukemia..., the patient took 24—42 grams Vitamin C per day... it is inconceivable that no one appears to have followed this up... without the scurvy, leukemia may be a relatively benign, non fatal condition. I wrote a paper... in an attempt to have the therapy clinically tested... I sent it to 3 cancer journals and 3 blood journals... it was refused by all... Two without even reading it."

~ Irwin Stone, Ph.D.

• "Cot-death is no longer a problem of clinical medicine, but is one of medical politics. We have long had the knowledge and experience as to how these unnecessary deaths can be avoided. In the meantime, to prevent your off-spring from becoming a SIDS statistic just make sure that its daily intake of ascorbate from conception on is sufficient. Under this regime the neonate is so robust and healthy that there has never been a case of SIDS among these ascorbate-corrected infants, not even a case of respiratory distress during birth."

~ Archie Kalokerinos, MBBS, PhD, FAPM

• "Many viral infectious diseases have been cured and can continue to be cured by the proper administration of Vitamin C. Yes, the vaccinations for these treatable infectious diseases are completely unnecessary when one has access to proper treatment with Vitamin C. And, yes, all the side effects of vaccinations... are also completely unnecessary since the vaccinations do not have to be given in the first place with the availability of properly dosed vitamin C."

~ Thomas Levy, MD, JD

• "Amazingly, vitamin C has actually already been documented in the medical literature to have readily and consistently cured both acute polio and acute hepatitis, two viral diseases still considered by modern medicine to be incurable."

~ Thomas E. Levy, MD, JD

*"Discovery consists of seeing what
everybody has seen and thinking
what nobody has thought."*
~ ALBERT VON SZENT-GYORGY

LONGEVITY PRINCIPLE #9
If there is to be a change, people must resist the fear of change and drive it.

WHY DID WE STOP THERE?

Events in the first half of the twentieth century could have altered the course of medical history but much research into nutrition slowed down in the late 40s. Some speculate that with World War II, the focus shifted to surgical advances to save our soldiers. Every one of us probably knows someone who was saved by the skillful hands of a surgeon and surgical advances were necessary at that time. Some speculate that with the discovery of penicillin, the focus shifted from prevention to eradication of germs; unfortunately, one of the consequences are "super bugs" that do not respond to antibiotic treatment. Just one year after the introduction of penicillin, some staph had become resistant to it. By the 1970s, almost 80 percent of staph was resistant to penicillin. Methicillin was introduced as the new antibiotic for staph, and now people are terrified of both community associated Methicillin Resistant *Staphylococcus Aureus* (CA-MRSA), or even worse, hospital associated (HA-MRSA) that has developed in the last 30 years.

Today, we have more faith in synthetic pharmaceutical drugs than we do in God's drugstore and our body's ability to heal itself. What keeps us locked in this pattern of thinking and acting when all the evidence says we should change? Why do we resist change?

Linus Pauling, Ph.D., a two time Nobel Prize winner, created the field of ortho-molecular science. *Ortho* means "correct" and "*molecular*" represents a molecule. A molecule is made of atoms. One atom cannot be defined as an "apple atom," or a "skin atom," but atoms combine to make a molecule, which is the smallest part of a whole that retains the characteristics of the whole, so you could see an apple molecule, or a skin molecule. The ideology of ortho-molecular science is that healthy nutrition, removing toxins such as junk food and customized nutrition, based on one's genetics, will lead to optimal health. Pauling stated that, "The current recommended daily allowance will prevent death. Where is the recommended daily allowance to prevent disease and create excellent health?"

RDA or ODA?

Should we seek the recommended daily allowance (RDA) of nutrients to keep us from being sick, or the *optimum* daily allowance (ODA) to help us thrive? For instance, the recommended daily allowance of vitamin C is 60 milligrams (mg) per day. Additionally, certain conditions increase our need for vitamin C.

For instance, passive smoke increases your need for vitamin C by 12 percent. (4) What's interesting is that all mammals on the planet, except four (including humans, guinea pigs and fruit bats), produce their own vitamin C—two to 20 grams of vitamin C for every 154 pounds of body weight. One gram is 1000 milligrams, yet our RDA is only 60mg? The good news is that although we do not produce vitamin C, we are better at recycling it than the other mammals that produce vitamin C. In prehistoric days, man populated tropical regions and ate a diet high in vitamin C. As a result, we lost our ability to produce vitamin C because it was so abundant in our diets. When humans left the tropical regions for other regions, disease began. Since humans are 99 percent genetically the same as chimpanzees, do humans need to take two to 20 grams of vitamin C per day? Pauling stated, "If you get the common cold, you do not take enough vitamin C."

The reality is that the RDA tells us what we need to keep from dying—but how much do we need to thrive? Richard Mather, Ph.D., analyzed a paper published by the National Academy of Sciences concerning a risk model for establishing an upper intake level of nutrients. Dr. Malther was horrified that the purpose of the paper was to "protect" citizens from self-medicating with nutraceuticals. A nutraceutical is a nutritional supplement of proven therapeutic value. For instance, pulmonary function can be improved in asthmatics by as much as 20 percent with vitamin C supplementation. The paper recommended limiting our access to these nutraceuticals or limiting the doses that we have access to.

OB/GYNs and other physicians state they were not aware of the protective effect of folic acid until 1992, when the U.S. Public Health Service recommended all pregnant women should consume 400 mcg of folic acid a day. In reality, folic acid deficiency had been linked to neural tube defects for more than 30 years. The first double blind studies showing a protective effect of folic acid supplementation were performed in the early 80s. (5) It took 12 years to state publicly that folic acid deficiency is linked to neural tube defects or 80 years to announce that butter is healthier than lard, and 250 years to offer liquids containing vitamin C to the Scottish Navy.

Why do we wait, especially if changes won't create harm? Why do we yell quackery when we hypothesize and offer cause and effect observations? A paradigm shift has occurred. What is a paradigm shift? It is a one time truth or concept that is no longer true. Many truthful observations have been made by both brilliant and mediocre people. The world was once considered flat, and a mediocre mathematician simply observed different angles of shadows cast at noon in different cities on the town wells. He calculated that the only conclusion to the variance was curvature of the earth, which he predicted within a few meters. His name was Eratosthenes and he was ridiculed. Dr. Lind was ridiculed. Semmelweiss was ridiculed. Linus Pauling was ridiculed because he was a Ph.D. and not an M.D. I am here to share common sense and cause and effect medicine. Is it all right to ask questions? Is it all right to make hypotheses? Come with me and ask yourself, "Does this make sense?" I often wonder whether I will be ridiculed?

Debi's Dialogue

I hope that you become very angry after reading this and other literature that proposes preventing the public from buying therapeutic doses of nutritional supplements such as Co-Enzyme Q10, (CoQ10) or other powerful antioxidants such as oligomeric proanthocyanidin complex (OPC).

Co-Q10 depletion has been shown in patients taking some statin drugs. Additionally, CoQ10 has been shown to be a vital antioxidant for heart health.

OPC's are clinically shown to pass the blood barrier in people with ADHD helping to improve concentration. OPC's are also shown to improve the ability to focus, naturally reduce inflammation and act as a natural antihistamine along with many other health benefits!

Can you imagine not being able to buy vitamin C for fear that we are self medicating while Prilosec, Claritin, Benadryl or Ibuprofen sits alongside the bubble gum at the checkout line along with numerous other "OTC?" Medications?

Are we not already self-medicating? Please! Do you want the only supplemental choice to be OTC drugs?

CHAPTER

10

Medical Hatfield's
vs. McCoy's

*"Human beings, the potentially highest form of
life expression on this planet, have built the vast
pharmaceutical industry for the central purpose of
poisoning the lowest form of life on the planet–germs!
One of the biggest tragedies of human civilization is
the precedence of chemicals over nutrition."*

~ Dr. Richard Murray

Disease is exactly that: DIS-ease. Ease is balance. How do you achieve absolute balance? Can you imagine not being afraid of the latest germ or disease? We do not catch disease; we make disease. Do maggots make garbage? Do germs make disease? We create disease with unhealthy food, drink and lifestyle choices. In some instances, we have no choice as we are presented with toxic chemicals in our water, air and food.

*What if germs did not
cause disease, but germs
were the result of disease?*

You've probably heard of Louis Pasteur, but have you heard of Antoine Béchamp?

Louis Pasteur was a French chemist. Pasteur's main theory is known as the "Germ Theory of Disease." This theory is the cornerstone of immunology. Germ theory claims that certain microorganisms cause disease. In the first chapter of forever young and vibrant, you will learn that the current practice of medicine is all about eradicating these microorganisms with vaccines and antibiotics. (2)

Antoine Béchamp was a scientist in France at the same time as Pasteur. Béchamp believed that small organisms were responsible for illness. However, these small organisms or germs were the *result* of illness, not the cause! Pasteur was known as an ambitious and opportunistic self promoter. He took part of Béchamp's research and publicized it as his own, leaving out the idea that germs were a function of disease, not the cause. Pasteur went on to profit from Germ Theory by identifying substances to destroy germs; hence the concepts of immunizations and antibiotics were born. To understand some of the basic differences between the medical Hatfield's and McCoy's, we must understand mono-morphism versus pleomorphism. This may seem complicated, but I will summarize after the definition is given.

Mono-morphism (one-form) means that a fixed organism, one that is *unchanging*, causes disease. This idea is the foundation of allopathic (traditional) Western medicine. It would make sense—if it were true. Once we identify the fixed organism, we can learn how to attack it, destroy it and eliminate disease. But as we all know, a bacteria develops resistance to antibiotics. How does this happen? *It changes*. Therefore, it cannot be fixed—or one form.

For many years, this ideology has made quacks out of those in the homeopathic medical profession who argued that the goal is not to eradicate disease but to create a terrain, (the body) that is balanced and healthy, so germs will not thrive. A trillion-dollar-a-year business thrives to eradicate the germ, led by the pharmaceutical companies, and includes the Food and Drug Administration (FDA), many insurance companies, the National Institutes of Health (NIH) and even the Centers for Disease Control and Prevention (CDC).

Pleomorphism (many-forms) differs from the ideology of monomorphism. In pleomorphism, the idea is that a tiny life form represents a time of change. For example, bacteria can change into yeast, yeast to fungus, fungus to mold. That may be controversial, but what is true is that microbes have been around since the dawn of the earth and are found in amber billions of years old. Microbes are the first life of our planet. What we now know is that microbes evolve rapidly, more rapidly than humans do, and adapt rapidly to a changing environment. Moreover, in every living thing are microbes that can change to be helpful or harmful depending on our health. If we are healthy, microbes produce substances that are healthy for us. It is the chicken and the egg, which comes first? Microbes will adapt to their surroundings faster than humans can adapt. Therefore, if our body is being poisoned with sugars, chemicals and drugs, the microbes will adapt to survive in this new terrain. Microbes emit substances; the healthier our body, the more beneficial the microbe. But if we are sick, microbes can change to produce substances that can be harmful.

It is interesting to me that science understands that most viruses cannot be killed with our current medications where bacteria can. A virus is considered not living but rather a sac of genetic material that will enter a cell and basically "reprogram it.'" Bacteria are considered living microorganisms so we have created drugs to kill the bacteria. Unfortunately, bacteria adapt and change to drugs. Again bacteria evolve much faster than humans do.

HATFIELD'S AND MCCOY'S

One school of thought is that to eradicate germs is to eradicate disease. The other believes that we must create a terrain (our bodies) where germs cannot thrive. Béchamp stated that bacteria could change forms. For instance, rod shaped bacteria could become spherical; or yeast could become mold, meaning that tiny organisms can adapt and change for the better or worse based on our health. Pasteur disagreed. In 1914, Madame Victor Henry

of The Pasteur Institute confirmed that Béchamp
was correct and that Pasteur was wrong. No one
can fully discredit Pasteur's work. As noted in the
1926 English translation of "The Life of Pasteur,"
by René Vallery-Radot, of Pasteur's last days:

> *"How willingly they would have given a moment of their
> lives to prolong his, those thousands of human beings whose
> existence had been saved by his methods; sick children,
> women in lying in hospitals, patients operated on in
> surgical wards, victims of rabid dogs saved from hydrophobia,
> and so many others protected against the infinitesimally
> small! But, whilst visions of those living beings passed
> through the minds of his family, it seemed as if Pasteur
> already saw those dead ones who, like him, had preserved
> absolute faith in the Future Life."*

Some argue that Pasteur renounced his life's
work on his deathbed, stating that Pasteur said,
"Bernard is correct. The bacteria are nothing. The
soil is everything." They say Pasteur was revealing
to the world that his Germ Theory of Disease
was concocted and false. Yet, the same people
who claim that Pasteur renounced his life's work
are the same who think Semmelweiss was right.
Semmelweiss was the one who argued that hand

washing between surgeries would lower death rates in hospitals. The odd thing is Semmelweiss was right about washing hands to kill the very germs they argue Pasteur renounced! Often there is truth on both sides of an argument.

The idea that the "soil is everything" means that the most important message our doctors can share with the public is *"to make our bodies so healthy that germs will not want to grow there." Germs invade already weakened bodies.* Don't be afraid of germs. When Pasteur said the "soil is everything" he meant that it was more important to strengthen the body (healthy food, environment and thoughts) than to attempt to destroy germs. This does not discount the reality and danger of microorganisms. Rather, it introduces the concept that some organisms are rendered ineffective in a specific environment. It seems we could approach health from both perspectives. One perspective is removing the microorganisms to the best of our ability through improved hygiene and another perspective is creating an ideal "soil," or body, where the organism does not thrive. Creating a healthy lifestyle includes adding exercise, a diet rich with fresh water, fruits and vegetables, good fats and lean meats as well as a lifestyle that includes more laughter and less stress. It is not an either/or—it is both!

PRESENT DAY - MICROBE RESEARCH

The study of microbes is becoming a hot topic. J. Craig Venter, a biologist named one of *Time Magazine's* Top 100 most influential people in 2007 and 2008, is the founder of the Institute for Genomic Research. Venter made huge contributions to the decoding of the human genome. Venter has just traveled the world, taking sea samples to find the DNA of the earth! What DNA is this? DNA of the smallest form of life—microbes! (3) There are tens of millions of microbes present in the sea that differ based on location, temperature, pH, depth and so on. Microbes are the smallest form of life and can produce toxins or medicinal substances. Microbes are what make up the probiotics that live in our intestinal area. For every cell in the body, there are at least 10 microbes, trillions upon trillions that act like pharmacies, producing both beneficial and toxic substances. It is time to understand these tiny creatures and how they affect our health because our life depends on it.

Our first inoculation comes from our mother but is made of these special, tiny microbes.

A scientist was commissioned to reproduce seawater for a Sea World-type exhibit. That would be easy, wouldn't it? The scientist analyzed the components of seawater and reproduced it, but when the fish were put in the water, they died. Had he done something wrong? He tried again, and again the fish died. The third time, the scientist added a small percent of real seawater and the fish lived. Could it be that there is more that we have not identified than what has been identified in our world? Could it be that tiny microbes that exist everywhere are vital to life? If this is the case, then wouldn't it make sense that microbes influence their surrounding environment? Science has studied every system in the body, and the function of cells—but if for every cell in the body, there are 10 microbes, wouldn't it be prudent to pay closer attention to these microbes? What if these microbes directly impacted our overall health? The origin of these microbes begins with the initial inoculation during the birthing process and is affected by foods and our environment. Remember, these microbes evolve and change far faster than humans do. As Venter maps the DNA of the sea, he looks toward his next project—studying the relationship between changes in human microbes and disease. I am excited to see this research. You are on the cutting edge of knowledge as you see the profound relationship between your health and your ability to absorb and assimilate nutrition. But the ability to absorb and assimilate nutrition is influenced by the microbes within your body and within the intestinal area. Since we have little knowledge of these microbes, their importance or their function, we have—in ignorance—negatively impacted the growth and development of the microbial population within our body, which affects our health.

Is This Also Happening In Our World?

I am reminded of the Great Barrier Reef. A report by The University of Queensland warned that damage to the reef would cost the economy $6.3 billion and more than 12 thousand jobs by 2020. (4) The Great Barrier Reef is dying off at an astounding rate. Much is to blame, including the rise in ocean temperatures, the abundance of fertilizer that has entered the ocean—changing the ocean's pH at this location—and an assault of microorganisms on the reef. (3) Certain microorganisms may have always been present, but simply could not thrive in the balanced pH. When the pH is disrupted, these once innocuous organisms can now thrive and destroy the more beneficial organisms the reef needs to thrive. Additionally, present day microorganisms are adapting and changing to their new environment. As they adapt to the new environment, they emit substances to 'maintain' their surroundings which kills off other beneficial microorganisms. There is a negative exponential effect. This can also be seen in our own intestinal area, with a dramatic effect on our immune system.

Many new diseases are affecting our world's reefs. One example is White Plague Type II, a potential bacterial pathogen, which has been recently identified by Kim Ritchie of the University of North Carolina and Dr. Garriet Smith. The bacterium is a newly discovered species and may represent an entire new classification. (5) It seems to me that as we poison our environment and our body, existing bacteria are adapting to thrive in this now toxic environment, creating an exponential effect creating further damage. Bacteria in the ocean are adapting to the temperature changes and the poisons being dumped; these new bacteria cause more damage because they thrive in the now toxic environment! Bacteria in our body are also adapting to changes, and the new bacteria will want more of the same, so they will participate by secreting chemicals to promote and support their new toxic environment.

As we change the ecology of the body,
The bacteria will change for
the better or worse to thrive
in the new environment.

Dr. Joel Robbins has served as a consultant to the U.S. Air Force and NATO for fighter pilot wellness training and is sought after for his successful wellness programs. (6) Dr. Robbins teaches that two conditions must be present in order for disease germs to enter the body or develop in living tissue. First, something must have already weakened the body before the germ enters. Second, there must be acidic debris present in the tissue for the germs to live on. Neither germs nor parasites can exist in a balanced acid-alkaline environment.

Many things can weaken the body, but the main thing is low oxygen—another reason to stop smoking and begin exercising! An acidic state can be caused by poor food choices, such as sugars or eating too much meat. But it is also brought about when the intestinal area is out of balance. I show in forever young and vibrant how an overly acidic body caused by poor food choices can reduce oxygen delivery to the cells and lead to cancer.

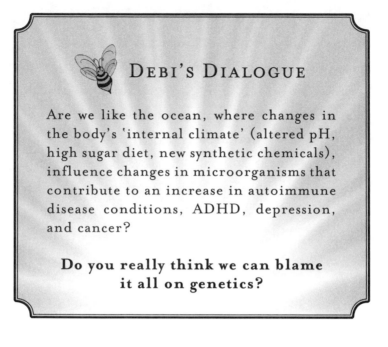

DEBI'S DIALOGUE

Are we like the ocean, where changes in the body's 'internal climate' (altered pH, high sugar diet, new synthetic chemicals), influence changes in microorganisms that contribute to an increase in autoimmune disease conditions, ADHD, depression, and cancer?

Do you really think we can blame it all on genetics?

The Role of the Stomach

"Every patient carries her or his own doctor inside."
~ ALBERT SCHWEITZER

Though I was and am impressed with doctors' knowledge, I knew they did not have all of the answers, so I decided to take personal responsibility for my health. When I had my "bumper sticker moment" and began journaling food and behavior, I was more convinced that it was not as simple as, "we are what we eat." We were already eating a well balanced diet, and we had incorporated exercise to get oxygen into our bodies. We were eating a diet rich in fruits and veggies and low in sugar to keep our body's pH in a neutral state. We were adopting activities to learn how to relax, meditate, dance or whatever it took to de-stress. I then looked at nutrition globally, studying the origins and evolution of medicine and I became frustrated. It seems that from every direction, we are told to take medicines or have surgeries, when little attention is paid to restoring and maintaining optimal health. I know fifty people who start with one drug that becomes two, three and more, for every one person who took a medication one time and was better. I needed to start over. As I looked at Joshua's behavior after eating the peanut butter, I knew there was a connection with his gastrointestinal tract. I could see dramatic changes in behavior based on what he would eat.

LONGEVITY PRINCIPLE #10
The gut trains the immune system.

❋

I was convinced that with all of our amazing discoveries, that even with the miracles of medicine, we were still missing something. I knew there was a breakdown somewhere and I was convinced it was more than diet. My great grandparents lived into their late 90's and they lived on flour and pig fat! My grandmother's coffee was more like tar than liquid. It had to be more than what we eat. You will find this hard to believe, but my great grandfather died in the 1970's from... complications from.... falling down a hill leaving his outhouse in Western Virginia—at the age of 98! They smoked. They ate whatever they had and they didn't go to a gym. And stress? Depended on how clean the outhouse was, I guess. I studied Joshua's signature and the change that occurred after feeding him peanut butter. I was left with one conclusion. The first point of entry of the peanut butter was the gastrointestinal tract. So I became a student of this part of the body. Let us take a close look at the process called digestion.

*Is it as simple as –
"We are what we eat?"*

DIGESTION

There are six processes of digestion that include saliva, mucus, enzymes, hydrochloric acid (HCL), bicarbonate and bile.   Enzymes are secreted in the mouth, stomach and small intestines. Saliva delivers enzymes in the mouth. Mucus protects the stomach lining. HCL lowers the pH of the stomach activating gastric enzymes and additional enzymes, bicarbonate and bile are needed for digestion and absorption in the small intestines.

Chapters 11 and 12 discuss processes that occur in the stomach and the small intestines. This chapter will discuss the movement of food and liquid, lubrication of food and bodily secretions, and the mechanical breakdown of proteins and in part, the initial digestion of carbohydrates in the mouth. Chapter 12 will discuss the mechanical breakdown of carbohydrates and fats in the small intestines and the further processing of protein bi-products as well as true lactose intolerance and beneficial bi-product created by probiotics. Additionally, the absorption of nutrients will be presented. It is important to understand this process because disease results when an intestinal imbalance exists. People who are sick and tired want to address the health of the intestinal tract.

The digestive process begins in the mouth and is complete when the food is evacuated at the other end. This long tube, or *lumen*, although inside you, is the outside of your body. Think of being inside out. Another name for this tube is the alimentary canal (AC). The AC protects your "real" insides from foreign invaders. Your "real" insides are your lymphatic tissue, blood and cells. Food in your stomach and intestines remains "outside" your body as it has not yet entered the blood and cells. Therefore, we digest all of our food *extracellularly*, or outside of our cells. Digestion occurs in the stomach and also in the intestinal area. Once food is digested, it is then safely able to enter the blood and ultimately the cells. There are two kinds of secretions in our body, exocrine and endocrine. Exocrine glands secrete externally through a duct, such as sweat, saliva and digestive juices. Endocrine glands secrete hormones directly into the blood. So any secretion within the lumen is actually outside of the body, kind of like sweat. A lumen is a hollow tube. The arteries are a lumen, and so are the intestines. For this discussion, I will use the words lumen and intestines interchangeably.

Think of your salivary secretions just before eating cotton candy. (1) Your mouth begins to water. When you eat, saliva is secreted and contains enzymes. Saliva is an exocrine secretion just like sweat. Again, exocrine secretions occur "outside" of your body although inside your mouth. Enzymes break the food into smaller particles that can be safely absorbed into the cell. It's up to the intestinal wall to select what enters the body. Don't think that because you put the food in your mouth and it disappears, that it's inside the body. It hasn't reached your "insides" until it has passed through the intestinal wall and into the lymph and blood stream. Remember, the lymph is part of the lymphatic system and the intestinal wall is related to the Gut-Associated Lymphoid Tissue (GALT). Swollen lymph nodes show infection. The lymph is throughout the body and captures foreign invaders. It utilizes white blood cells to destroy these foreign invaders in a properly functioning immune system. The gut trains the immune system.

Linus Pauling said, "To achieve optimal wellness, a person must achieve optimal concentrations of nutrition in every cell of the body." Clearly, there's more to it than "we are what we eat." We are also what we absorb and assimilate. In order to absorb and assimilate optimally, we must first have a properly functioning intestinal area. Proper intestinal functioning includes a healthy intestinal wall that decides what is transported into the blood stream and this begins with effective digestion. Digestion requires optimal pH and digestive enzyme secretions. Going back to the cotton candy example, saliva is an exocrine secretion that contains enzymes. Amylase is an enzyme that digests carbohydrates. Since amylase is in the saliva, and cotton candy is made of simple carbohydrates, then cotton candy melts in your mouth. The sugar is digested immediately. Since digestion begins in the mouth, then Mom was right—we really should chew our food thoroughly. We moisten the food and chew it and the resulting lump of food is called a bolus. This bolus is pushed through the esophagus by a process called peristalsis. Peristalsis is rhythmic contractions that automatically push the bolus through the esophagus to the stomach. Peristalsis also pushes feces through the colon and finally out through the anus.

DIGESTIVE ENZYME SECRETION AND pH

There are more exocrine glands in the lining of the stomach and these are called gastric glands. At least nine kinds of glands in the stomach secrete fluids, enzymes and acids with several distinct purposes. The main jobs of the stomach are storage and the beginning of protein digestion.

What is important to understand is that when you eat scrambled eggs and toast, for example, the toast starts to digest in your mouth because the bread contains carbohydrates; the eggs do not digest in the mouth since the eggs contain protein. Protein is digested in the stomach. So, once the eggs and toast leave your mouth and enter your stomach, the toast is digested very little, if at all, because amylase, the digestive enzyme for starches, is in essence deactivated or "turned off" in the stomach's very acidic environment. Enzymes are activated at different and specific pH levels. The pH level of the mouth is around 7, or fairly neutral, which activates amylase. The pH of the stomach is ideally between 1 and 3. Certain enzymes are "turned on and turned off" based on the pH of the environment they're in. Carbohydrates primarily digest in the mouth and again in the small intestines. Many people think all digestion occurs in the stomach, but this is not true. The stomach's main purpose is not to digest carbohydrates, but to digest proteins. Your breakfast toast will remain relatively unchanged in the stomach and will not digest further until it enters the small intestines. In fact, a great deal of digestion also occurs in the small intestines.

PROTEIN DIGESTION AND pH

If you remember our discussion of antibodies and antigens in Chapter 2, then you recall that an antigen is a foreign protein and an antibody "tags" the protein for attack. It is important then to remember that the stomach's job is to break proteins down into smaller and safer components. This is very important in decreasing immune reactions. In order to do this, the stomach's pH must be perfect. The following table will give you an idea of the pH values of common substances. You can buy pH test strips that you place on your tongue to test salivary pH. Typically, salivary pH is a good indication of your overall body pH and health. The strips reactions to pH and color changes that occur differ according to each manufacturer's color scheme. For instance, some tests show yellow and gold as more acidic, green as more neutral and blue as more alkaline.

Typical pH values

Stomach Acid	1.5-2.0
Lemon Juice	2.4
Cola	2.5
Vinegar	2.9
Healthy Vagina	3.8-4.5
Coffee	5.0
Healthy Skin	5.0
Heathy Feces	6-7
Pure Water	7.0
Healthy Saliva	6.6-7.3
Blood	7.4
Seawater	8.0
Baking Soda	9.0
Milk of Magnesia	10.0
Housecleaning Ammonia	11.5
Bleach	12.0

The most important point to remember is the number values. Either extreme of pH can be caustic. Numbers below seven are considered acidic, and numbers above 7 are considered alkaline. I regularly use a pH test strip, much like people with diabetes test their blood sugar.

Again, what is most important is the pH number.
Please remember that the colors you are looking
for will depend on the test kit you buy. I tear off
about a one-inch strip and place it on my tongue
for a second. You want the test strip to come out
neutral. Wait at least two hours after eating. Place
the strip on your tongue and thoroughly wet the
strip. For most tests, if you do the test immediately
after brushing your teeth, the strip will come very
alkaline (my test strip shows alkaline as purple).
This is not accurate but is a fun party trick. When
the pH test strip is neutral or around 7, it indicates
that my body tissue and blood are in a neutral
state, which is ideal. A more acidic state can be
indicative of an imbalance or disease. Believe it or
not, people who are not well will place the strip on
their tongue and it will come out below 6.0 which
may indicate a mineral deficiency. I remember
when my Dad had cancer, I placed a pH test strip
on his tongue and it came out at 4.5. People with
cancer often have a severe problem with body tissue
pH being too acidic. I talk a great deal about pH
and the negative implications to the body that is
continually trying to adjust an overly acidic state
in my second book, forever young and vibrant.

Pathogens in the body thrive in an acidic state. It is interesting that the ideal state of the stomach is acidic. The ideal state of the intestines is slightly acidic. The ideal pH of the skin is slightly acidic, yet the ideal pH of the body tissue is more neutral. When the pH of the intestines or the stomach is less acidic, or more neutral to alkaline, the body tissue responds by testing more acidic. Remember, every part of the body is designed for a specific and optimum pH.

HCL and Digestion

Hydrochloric acid (HCL) is secreted in the stomach. Every person secretes HCL for digestion. As we age, we produce less HCL. Hydrochloric acid by itself does not digest protein. The digestive enzyme pepsin separates proteins into smaller polypeptide chains. Since pepsin digests proteins and we are made of proteins, the body first secretes pepsinogen, a precursor to pepsin. This means that when pepsinogen meets hydrochloric acid in the stomach, the pepsinogen becomes pepsin. Since pepsinogen and hydrochloric acid are secreted by different cells, they don't come into contact with each other until they meet in the stomach cavity. This is good because we don't want to digest ourselves!

The body will attack a protein, but not shorter chains of polypeptides made of amino acids. Proteins can produce an antibody reaction, where shorter chains of polypeptides will not trigger an immune response. If the stomach's pH is not perfect, then digestive enzymes will not be activated. How can you digest proteins fully if you are taking antacids or various medications that can alter your stomach's pH? Again, enzymes work completely in an optimum pH specific for each enzyme.

When I was at Portland State University, I had a science lab on digestion. We took several test tubes and placed in them hydrochloric acid, pepsin (the enzyme that breaks apart proteins) and meat. We then altered each test tube. We added water to one. We changed the temperature of another. And in the third, we changed the pH. The change in digestion was basically nonexistent in the first two tubes, but in the third tube, where we'd changed the pH, digestion ceased completely.

Stomach Mucus and the Impact of Drugs

The stomach also secretes mucus as a protection

from secreted acid and enzymes. Here is something to consider regarding stomach mucus production; many people buy NSAIDS or non-steroidal anti-inflammatories. NSAIDS block the pathways causing inflammation. Unfortunately, the same pathways also cause mucus production and gastric motility. Therefore, if a person takes a great deal of NSAIDS, especially on an empty stomach, they risk damage to their GI tract. In addition to reducing pain, the drugs reduce gastric mucus production that protects the stomach leaving people vulnerable to gastric upset or even worse, ulcers. If you are in a chronically inflamed state that requires months of NSAIDS, I encourage you to read forever young and vibrant to learn how correcting your body pH, adding Omega 3 and specific antioxidants can greatly reduce inflammation and thus, pain.

Stomach pH and Antacids

Pepsinogen needs the stomach's low pH and hydrochloric acid in order to be converted into pepsin. Since this acidic pH range is also necessary for proper functioning of pepsin, a pH of 2.0 is optimum. It is thought that antacids not only change pH, but also interfere with the effectiveness of pepsin to break down proteins. Only in a perfect state can the digestive enzymes secreted by the stomach be activated to break the proteins into polypeptides. If you take a great deal of antacids and change the pH of your stomach from acidic to less than acidic, then how can your enzymes work properly? Stomach enzymes are only activated in a very acidic state. So hydrochloric acid doesn't actually digest food alone; it *prepares* food so enzymes can break the food down.

DANGER OF INCOMPLETELY DIGESTED PROTEINS

With all the prescribed and OTC antacids on the market, it is important you really understand what the stomach does. This is no longer a discussion just for doctors but for you, the consumer and citizen. Please understand that proteins in and of themselves are not dangerous. When they are separated in the stomach into smaller chains of polypeptides and released into the intestines, they are the building blocks our body needs for growth and repair. In the small intestines, another enzyme called peptidase breaks these polypeptide chains down into even smaller parts called amino acids. However, if this grand orchestra of digestion is impaired in any way and the proteins are not broken down, these "foreign" proteins are seen as dangerous "invaders" and must be attacked. Then we have some type of immune response to them. Therefore, if you are taking off the shelf - acid reducers what happens? Look back at the pH chart and ask, "if my stomach pH needs to be 1-3, and I take milk of magnesia with a pH of 10, can I digest my proteins?" Stomach enzymes are triggered to work only if the stomach's pH level is perfect!

Normally, the grand orchestra is perfectly balanced with the simultaneous release of hydrochloric acid and enzymes. But what happens if as we age, we have less of a secretion of hydrochloric acid, or enzymes or both? What happens if medications inhibit the release of these fluids? What happens if our culture makes it increasingly difficult for the stomach to do its job completely? Let's look at the consequences of undigested foods, toxins and undigested proteins entering our intestinal area.

GOOD ADVICE:

1. Obtain pH Test strips and check your salivary pH on a regular basis.
2. Strive for a salivary pH of 7.
   - forever young and vibrant includes food charts and methods to improve your body's pH.
3. Choose to eat at the table and focus on enjoying your food.
4. Avoid eating in front of the television or the computer.
5. Chew your food slowly.

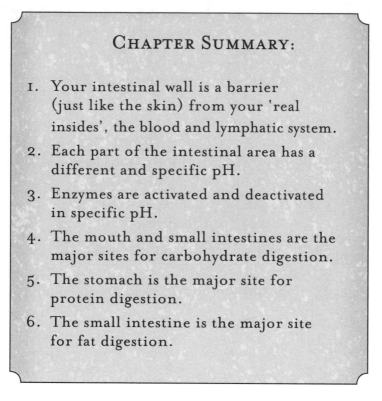

CHAPTER SUMMARY:

1. Your intestinal wall is a barrier (just like the skin) from your 'real insides', the blood and lymphatic system.

2. Each part of the intestinal area has a different and specific pH.

3. Enzymes are activated and deactivated in specific pH.

4. The mouth and small intestines are the major sites for carbohydrate digestion.

5. The stomach is the major site for protein digestion.

6. The small intestine is the major site for fat digestion.

DEBI'S DIALOGUE

Congratulations! You know more about what happens in the stomach than 90% of the people on the planet.

But why know this?

According to Dr. Michael Gershon, the gastrointestinal area is controlled by a 'second brain' and has its own nervous system. Why do you get 'butterflies' in your stomach or why do you feel nauseous when you are nervous? Have you ever had a 'gut reaction'?

There are more serotonin receptor sites in the intestinal area than in the brain. There are ten bacteria in the gut for every cell in the body. Half of the nerves of your body are located in the gut.

Our thoughts affect not only our brain, but also affect our gut.

CHAPTER

12

The Role of the Small Intestines

"As I see it, every day you do one of two things: build health or produce disease in yourself."
~ ADELLE DAVIS, DYSBIOSIS AND DISEASE

DYSBIOSIS AND DISEASE

Dysbiosis is a serious condition. Earlier I discussed that complete lack of vitamin C leads to a deadly disease caused scurvy. Years of a sub optimal dose of vitamin C will prevent scurvy but many other disease conditions result. Likewise, dramatic alterations to the intestinal flora can result in diseases such as irritable bowel disease, Crohn's disease, cancer and more. However, few discussions have addressed the consequences of long term imbalances in the intestinal flora. Dysbiosis is an imbalance in the intestinal flora and has been overlooked by the medical community as the cause of numerous disease states. The good news is that there are now thousands of clinical studies that support the seriousness of this condition. The initial development of the intestinal tract can dramatically impact a person's health for life. Additionally, a previously healthy individual may succumb to disease after experiencing significant changes in environmental or lifestyle factors. The key to staying healthy is in understanding the complex role of the intestines and then avoiding environmental or lifestyle changes that can have a negative effect on health.

If a person is optimally inoculated at birth, breast-fed, had solid food introduced after six months and cow's milk after one year, she may have a very healthy intestinal tract. Unfortunately, many substances assault the flora. Myecin antibiotics are known to kill 99 percent of all bacteria in the gut. If this happens and the person is not counseled about the effects of the drug, that person may go out in ignorance and eat just as they always have, not understanding that the integrity of their intestinal tract now, is similar to a newborn infant. It could take months or years to restore the integrity of the intestinal tract. (1) Additionally, antacids or H-2 blockers can impair the digestion of proteins. When this happens, intact proteins enter the duodenum which is not equipped for protein digestion. The protein will basically rot, releasing toxins into the GI tract and providing fuel for harmful pathogenic organisms. Additionally, as people age, the ability to produce HCL and enzymes becomes impaired. Protein digestion can become compromised, again leading to dysbiosis. Other drugs can contribute to dysbiosis including birth control pills, steroid drugs, anesthesia and cancer treatments such as chemotherapy and radiation. Of course, some people may not be able to avoid these treatments. Now is the time to educate the public on ways to avoid the gastrointestinal disturbances that will likely ensue.

THE SMALL INTESTINES

In a living person, the small intestines are ten feet long. There are three distinct sections of the small intestine, the duodenum which is about ten inches long, the jejunum which is three feet long and the ileum which is six feet long. Many articles report the intestines are 25 to 30 feet, but this would be found in a cadaver where flaccidity creates the difference in length.

The stomach pH is highly acidic and changes slightly, becoming less acidic, just before passing through the pyloric valve and entering the duodenum. The pyloric valve separates the contents of the stomach from the small intestines. The mouth and stomach have desirable and specific pH and so do the small intestines. Ideally, the pH of the duodenum is between five and six, the jejunum, between six and seven and the ileum pH is between seven and eight. (2) At the end of the ileum is the ileocecal valve and this juncture protects feces from backing into the small intestines. The colon pH is between six and seven and finally, the rectum's pH will have risen to between seven and eight. Why is all of this important? First, I wouldn't want my feces to have a pH of five! Ouch! Second, every part of the intestinal tract has a function with specific enzymes. Again, if the pH is not perfect, enzymes cannot work properly and if the intestinal tract is too alkaline, harmful pathogens will grow.

THE DIGESTION OF CARBOHYDRATES CONTINUES IN THE SMALL INTESTINES

Pepsin in the stomach digests proteins but not carbohydrates, so the toast we ate that is in the stomach may have been diluted, but digestion is dramatically diminished. Carbohydrates from the toast must be broken down into simpler sugars so the cells can absorb them for energy. Cells cannot absorb pieces of toast! The pancreas secretes many enzymes into the small intestines, in fact, this is where most nutritional absorption occurs. The stomach holds and processes the food and digests proteins. The small intestines continue digestion and absorption of nutrition from the food. The colon's main purpose is to remove leftover fluid water and waste from this process.

Two ducts enter the first part of the small intestine called the duodenum. One duct drains the gallbladder and the liver. The other duct drains the exocrine portion of the pancreas. Remember, exocrine secretions happen "outside" the body and are processes such as sweat and the production of saliva and digestive enzymes. Endocrine secretions happen "inside" the body, such as when the thyroid gland secretes thyroid hormone and the brain's pituitary gland secretes human growth hormone. The pancreas offers both exocrine and endocrine secretions. The pancreas's exocrine secretions are digestive enzymes secreted into the small intestines and the endocrine secretion is insulin, secreted into the bloodstream. (3)

The pancreas secretes enzymes that digest your toast or other carbohydrates. But how? Enzymes the pancreas secretes do not work in the same pH as the stomach. Therefore, bicarbonate (like baking soda) and bile (see fat digestion below) are secreted into the small intestines to alter the pH of the solution coming from the stomach. This new pH "turns off" pepsin, so protein digestion is halted and other enzymes are "turned on" to break down carbohydrates and fats and further break down the polypeptides into amino acids. It's clear that pH level is very important all along the digestive tract!

DIGESTION OF FAT OCCURS IN THE SMALL INTESTINES

Between meals, the liver makes bile, which is stored in the gallbladder and excreted into the small intestines to help break down fat. If you've vomited, then you may have seen and tasted a bitter yellow-green fluid. This is bile. Bile is made of cholesterol, bile salts and bilirubin. Bile salts help to break down fat and keep the cholesterol in the gallbladder in a liquid state. Bilirubin is a by-product of the natural breakdown of red blood cells and is part of the reason feces are brown. Great conversation for your next social engagement, huh? Gallstones can occur when there is too much cholesterol in the gallbladder or too little bile salts, allowing the cholesterol to harden into stones. When you eat food that contains fats, bile is secreted into the small intestines. Bile acts like Dawn dish-washing soap— it breaks the fat into smaller particles. Bile doesn't change the structure of fats; it just changes the size. Emulsification is the process of breaking the fat down into tiny droplets that are more easily digested and absorbed. Remember, vitamins such as vitamin A and vitamin E are fat soluble (made of fat) and are absorbed using this same mechanism. We want our gallbladders working if at all possible. This is why "fat blockers" for weight loss can be dangerous, because they block the absorption of very important fat soluble vitamins like vitamins A, E and D and even CoQ10. In fact, I read the box of a popular fat blocker sold at local drug stores and it recommends wearing dark pants the first few weeks in case you experience greasy, oily seepage! You will love forever young and vibrant where I offer simple ways to lose body fat, without having to worry about ...seepage!

The change of pH to a less acidic state stimulates digestion in the small intestines. Carbohydrates continue to digest and are reduced to simple sugars. Fats are broken down into smaller particles called mono-glycerides. As mentioned before, peptidase breaks down polypeptides (the bi-product of protein digestion in the stomach) into amino acids.

Absorption Sites

Final absorption and digestion occurs in the small finger-like projections of the small intestines called villi. The walls of the small intestines lined with finger-like projections are themselves lined with even smaller finger-like projections called microvilli. These projections increase the surface area of the intestines allowing for maximum absorption of nutrition. If you were to take the intestines and stretch it out, smoothing out the entire finger like projections until you had a flat surface, it would cover a tennis court. (3) In an earlier quote, it was mentioned that the lymphatic tissue of the intestines is the size of a football field whereas the lymphatic tissue from the rest of the body is the size of a door. Hopefully, you are beginning to see the tremendous importance of having a properly developed and functioning intestinal area. The surface area of the intestinal area is greater than the surface area of skin. Consider the intestinal surface area the size of a tennis court and the gut lymphatic tissue the size of a football field; it is no wonder that changes to these two structures can have tremendous impact on overall health.

PROBIOTICS

Throughout saving 'generation next', I have mentioned probiotics numerous times. Research shows some 200 to 500 different types of bacteria in the gut. Another term for probiotics is 'friendly bacteria.' The three most important 'friendly bacteria' are Lactobacillus acidophilus and Saccaromyces Boulardi, residing in the small intestines and Bifidobacterium bifidum (bifidus), residing in the large intestines. Many authors state that the small intestines are sterile and contain no bacteria, but this is not true. (4) In relation to the large intestines, the small intestines contain fewer probiotics, but the probiotics that are there serve many important functions. Microbes in the small intestines assist in the digestion and absorption of nutrients from carbohydrates, fats and proteins. Probiotics emit antibiotic like substances that protect against harmful pathogens. More importantly, friendly bacteria produce acids that help maintain a slightly acidic intestinal area. The low pH prevents harmful pathogens from thriving.

PROBIOTICS AND GALL STONES

Additionally, probiotics break down conjugated bile salts and bilirubin. Gall stones form when the solubility of bilirubin or cholesterol is exceeded. There are two different types of gallstones, pigment and cholesterol stones. Pigment bile stones come from an excess of bilirubin. If probiotics breakdown bilirubin (bi-product of red blood cells) then does taking a probiotic formulation reduce the pigment type gallstone? Yes!

PROBIOTICS AND LACTOSE INTOLERANCE

Lactobacillus acidophilus produce enzymes that degrade lactose (milk sugar). Lactose is a complex sugar called a disaccharide. A disaccharide is made of more than one simple sugar. Lactose is degraded by an enzyme called Lactase into glucose and galactose.

How many people do you know who are lactose intolerant? I didn't even ask if you have heard of it because it's all over the media with products such as Lactaid being advertised. Many people think they are lactose intolerant. Lactose is a sugar found in milk. Lactose digestion requires an enzyme our body normally produces called lactase. Lactase is found in the intestinal tract.

We've discussed how the intestinal tract has a variety of pH levels and that certain enzymes "turn off" and "turn on" according to pH level. Another way of looking at enzyme pH levels is to understand that specific enzymes have an optimum pH or a pH where they work best. The optimum pH for the lactase enzyme is 6.7. (5) Lactase is found predominantly in the jejunum (second portion of the small intestines). The natural pH of the jejunum is between six and seven, ideal for lactose digestion.   Beneficial bacteria secrete acids in the intestinal area lowering pH.   In fact, acidophilus could be referred to as 'acid loving' bacteria. When the intestinal tract has not been properly inoculated or colonized, the intestinal pH level is more alkaline. The enzyme that digests lactose works less efficiently at a pH level that is less than or greater than 6.7. Research shows that supplementing with acidophilus and bifidus bacteria may be *more helpful* than with lactase alone since probiotics reduce intestinal pH so the lactase you are taking can work. If a person takes a lactase supplement and the pH level of their intestines is elevated due to poor inoculation, overuse of medications, stress or even too much sugar, then the supplemental lactase can't work optimally. I wonder how many people are truly lactose intolerant? Maybe rather than producing less lactase, they simply have an intestinal area that is too alkaline due to a reduction in healthy intestinal bacteria thereby deactivating the lactase enzyme.

If you look up Lactobacillus and Lactose on the internet, you will find numerous pages citing one study published in the American Journal of Clinical Nutrition authored by Saltzmen, et al. in 1999 that says Lactobacillus acidophilus does not improve lactose intolerance. (6) Like many studies, you have to dig deeper. In fact, an earlier study published in the Journal of Nutrition, August, 1997 showed that Lactobacillus acidophilus actually produces the lactase enzyme and that supplementation is helpful for those deemed lactose intolerant. (7) How can two published studies arrive at opposite conclusions? In the study that showed improvement, subjects were given small, daily doses of milk along with the acidophilus. The study concluded that humans were created to consume milk for just a short time. Once a baby is weaned, over time, the ability to digest lactose is impeded. In fact, most seniors are lactose intolerant. However, if the individual continued to drink milk and probiotic acidophilus, then the incidence of lactose intolerance was reduced. The study that found Lactobacillus acidophilus ineffective against lactose intolerance did not give the subjects milk along with their probiotic. It seems we need both to counter normal loss of lactase. If a person lives in a culture that drinks milk for a lifetime AND has an abundance of Lactobacillus acidophilus, then, lactose intolerance is diminished. Again, the acidophilus modifies the intestinal pH so that the lactase enzyme can work in the optimal pH and produces lactase enzyme. The lactase enzyme is found on the surface of the brush borders of the microvilli and would be more susceptible to pH changes. Other disaccharidases (complex sugar enzymes) are deeper within the microvilli and may be less vulnerable to pH changes in the gut.

It is interesting that African-Americans have a higher incidence of hypertension (high blood pressure). Research shows that calcium intake can reduce hypertension, yet many minorities think they are lactose intolerant and avoid dairy products. (8) The unfortunate point is that our nation is directed to drink milk for calcium. What few people understand is that milk contains vitamin D2 which is not as efficient at aiding in calcium absorption as vitamin D3. D3 comes from the sun. Since African Americans have darker skin, they need longer in the sun to produce the necessary vitamin D3. Calcium absorption from milk is 28% compared to 41% from green leafy vegetables. I would highly suggest supplementing with isotonic calcium that includes vitamin D3 and eat an abundance of green leafy vegetables. I grew up in Hampton Virginia; it was not uncommon to see people loading their shopping carts with collard greens. Today, less people eat green, leafy vegetables, a good source of vitamin D; rather, shopping carts are filled with packaged and processed foods. Sunlight produces vitamin D3, yet people are advised to stay out of the sun. I wonder why for thousands and thousands of years, people in the sun did not get skin cancer! Calcium, green leafy vegetables, vitamin D3 and sunlight will be discussed in forever young and vibrant.

GUT-ASSOCIATED LYMPHOID TISSUE (GALT) TRAINS THE IMMUNE SYSTEM

As we've already discussed, the intestinal wall is an important barrier that selectively chooses what passes into the body. Microvilli feed into capillaries and are closely associated with the lymphatic tissue that makes up a large part of the immune system. The gut associated lymphatic tissue runs alongside the intestinal tract and is exposed in area called Peyer's patches (PP) that produce various immune cells. Research shows a direct correlation in the abundance of probiotics and the abundance of Peyer's patches. When the intestinal area is healthy, the lymphatic tissue, or GALT, responds normally to food we eat. When the gut is optimally developed, then probiotics are abundant and this creates an optimal pH state. When the pH is optimal, then pathogens cannot grow and enzymes work properly. Additionally, when there is an abundance of probiotics in the intestinal area and an abundance of prebiotics from oligosaccharides, there will be an abundance of the IgA antibody. The IgA antibodies will engulf bacteria and viruses and destroy them before the immune system "sees" them and begins an autoimmune response. Therefore, the presence of prebiotics, probiotics, and IgA antibodies create a healthy GALT. The healthy GALT participates in desensitizing the immune system. However, when the intestinal area is out of balance—either due to inefficient inoculation of good bacteria from mother, failure to fully to colonize the gut bacteria by introducing formula and solid foods too soon, or stress, high sugar and medications—then the intestinal wall never fully develops and neither does the GALT, which affects the immune system. We become hypersensitive to foods and our environment because with fewer IgA, the immune system sees far more foreign proteins and therefore becomes hyperactive. We want to be very careful about what enters our body. If the intestinal wall is affected, it becomes, in essence, more porous or immature (like a baby) becoming less selective to random particles. When inappropriate substances enter the blood and lymph systems an inappropriate immune response is the result. (4,5) Numerous drugs can affect the production of stomach acid, which can affect the activity of enzymes resulting in incompletely digested proteins entering the small intestines.

ISOTONIC IS THE BEST STATE FOR ABSORPTION OF NUTRIENTS

We have discussed digestion and we understand that proteins are broken down in the stomach. Carbohydrates begin to digest in the mouth. Carbs and fats are further broken down in the small intestines. The stomach also serves to dilute this solution of food called chyme (a soupy mixture), in the stomach, until it becomes *isotonic*. *Iso* (equal) *tonic* (tone) means "same tension." It means that two solutions have equal numbers of solutes. They have the same concentrations. However this does not always happen. If we eat a lot of food, the pyloric valve may open prematurely and allow chyme to enter the small intestines before the solution has been processed and becomes isotonic. The quantity of food in the stomach will dictate how soon the pyloric valve opens.

The ideal state for absorption of nutrients in the intestinal area is when the concentration of the solution in the lumen (the intestinal side) is the same as the concentration of the solution on the blood and lymphatic side (the other side of the intestinal wall).

Think of a glass of cold iced tea that is to be sweetened with sugar. You add a little sugar and it dissolves so you add more. You add more and more, until the sugar sinks to the bottom of the glass. When the sugar sinks to the bottom, the iced tea liquid is saturated with sugar solids. What you see is a relationship between solids (sugar) and liquids (iced tea). This relationship represents the density or pressure of the liquid. Therefore, isotonic means that different solutions have the same density (solids to liquid ratio). Your body also has a ratio of solids to liquid in the blood and lymph.

The body strives to maintain an equal balance on both sides of membranes—whether that membrane is the intestinal wall, or cell membrane does not matter. You will find the body wants to keep the ratio of solids to liquid the same on both sides of the intestinal wall and inside the body.

Why? Nutritional absorption occurs in the intestines WHEN the solution on the intestinal side is the same concentration as the solution on the blood side or isotonic. If the intestines receive food that is not properly diluted, or only partially digested, then the liquid that enters the intestines is more concentrated with solids than the liquid on the other side of the intestinal wall. Since your body wants to create an isotonic state first, before it will absorb nutrition, the intestines will bring water into the intestinal area from the other side of the intestinal wall, 'diluting' the solution and making that solution equal in its solids-to-liquid ratio as the blood. When chyme passes through the pyloric valve, the small intestines determine if the solution is hypertonic (overly concentrated), isotonic (perfect for absorption) or hypotonic (diluted). No nutrition will be absorbed until the solution is isotonic.

A process called segmentation occurs in the small intestines where opposing muscles contract, moving the mixture back and forth waiting for the isotonic solution to develop. If the solution is too concentrated, then water will move into the digestive tract, and you may have diarrhea. Numerous studies document the dangers of consuming high carbohydrate energy drinks while running a marathon or other vigorous activities. These drinks can be overly concentrated and when they enter the intestinal area, segmentation occurs and water is rapidly moved into the digestive tract while the solution is being made isotonic. Runners may feel pain and discomfort and it is not uncommon that a runner may take a detour and experience a bout of diarrhea. As the water moves into the digestive tract, minerals do as well, and the runner can actually experience dehydration. Conversely, if the chyme is overly diluted while the mixture is being processed during segmentation, water will move out of the intestinal area until the solution becomes isotonic and is ready for absorption.

However, when the solution that enters the intestinal area is the same concentration or pressure—isotonic—as the solution on the other side; then water will not move back and forth—*nutrients* will, and they will be absorbed more quickly. *Delivery of an isotonic solution to the small intestines is the best state for nutritional absorption.* If I choose to supplement, I want nutrition that is isotonic.

So before you worry about what's on your plate or what you eat, remember that digestion begins in your mouth and that proper pH levels in the stomach are vital for complete protein digestion. Three generations of high sugar diets, chemicals, preservatives, formulas with no oligosaccharides, antibiotics, stress, and over use of antibiotics have dramatically affected what we all take for granted, digesting our food. If we do not completely digest our proteins, then we may increase our risk for autoimmune disease. Additionally, the health of the intestinal area dictates the health of our Gut-Associated Lymphoid Tissue, which depends on probiotics and proper pH to operate effectively. In a mature GALT, the body's immune system is desensitized rather than hyperactive. Final digestion occurs in the small intestines and the best state of nutritional absorption is isotonic. To produce an isotonic solution from our stomach, we want to make sure our gastric pH level is optimal and we have sufficient digestive enzymes. Supplementing with digestive enzymes, prebiotics, probiotics and isotonic supplemental nutrition may be beneficial in individuals who do not have a fully mature GALT.

If you choose to supplement, make sure your supplementation is natural and in an isotonic state – most often a powder or liquid.

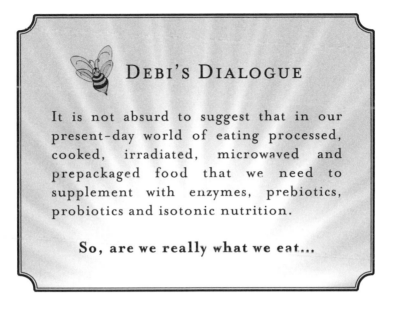

DEBI'S DIALOGUE

It is not absurd to suggest that in our present-day world of eating processed, cooked, irradiated, microwaved and prepackaged food that we need to supplement with enzymes, prebiotics, probiotics and isotonic nutrition.

So, are we really what we eat...

Giving Your Child the Gift of Optimal Health

"For myself I am an optimist – it does not seem to be much use being anything else."
~ SIR WINSTON CHURCHILL

The maturity of an infant's immune system depends on the maturity of the Gut-Associated Lymphoid Tissue, which depends on the development and maturity of the infant's intestinal bacterial mix or ecology. Development of this intestinal ecology depends on the infant's initial maternal inoculation from the baby's mother and further development of this bacterial ecology based on feeding habits and environmental exposure. Further development of the flora involves foods eaten, the body's ability to digest and absorb the nutrition and genetic variations that determine how nutrients are utilized at a cellular level.

Our society has spent the last 20 years focusing on what should go on our plates—good fats vs. bad fats, complex vs. refined carbs, fish and poultry vs. red meat, nine servings of fruits and vegetables each day, eight glasses of water each day, one glass of red wine and on and on. But how many of you eat fairly well but still have issues with fatigue, depression or obesity? I have seen people spend three months adopting new and healthy habits and have quit because they did not see enough of a change. I suggest that these people are unaware that they have an intestinal tract that is keeping them from feeling great. Let's assume that you follow the fundamentals of good eating. What remains is what happens once the food enters the body—something that has been taken for granted until recently. Most nutritional absorption occurs in the small intestines. Since the intestinal tract is intimately related to the immune system, it is important to understand how the GALT relates to the intestinal tract.

The GALT drives the immune system. How

the body breaks down, digests and absorbs nutrition will determine whether the immune system becomes hyperactive or hypo-active. An intestinal tract that is not operating optimally allows more toxins and undigested proteins into the body creating a burden for the liver. In forever young and vibrant, I discuss how a burdened liver increases free radicals and oxidative stress further negatively affecting the immune system.

LONGEVITY PRINCIPLE #11
The colonization of the bacteria in the infant's intestinal area is the dawning of the infant's immune system.

I'm going to appeal to your sense of humanity before we get back into the science. Since the mother inoculates the infant during the birthing process and since the colonization of the bacteria in the infant's intestinal area directly affects the immune system, as a mother, would you change some behaviors before having a baby? If that were true, then what if within the past 60 years, we

have introduced into our society substances and
lifestyles that have negatively affected a mother's
ability to inoculate her baby, thereby negatively
affecting the baby's immune system's ability to
protect itself? (1,2)

When a baby is properly inoculated as a result of being
born through an abundantly populated birth canal and
being breast-fed from a mother with a healthy balance
of bacteria, then the baby will have a gut pH level of
approximately 5.1 to 5.4 during its first six weeks that
is dominated by a probiotic (friendly bacteria) called
bifidobacteria. (3) There are 500 kinds of bacteria
in the intestinal area and bifidobacteria is one of the
most dominant. Bifidobacteria infantus is found
in babies. A research study conducted by Wang and
Gibson in Cambridge, UK introduced bad bacteria
such as, E. coli, Salmonella, Listeria, Campylobacter
and Shigella, as well as Vibrio Cholerae to cultures of
the good bacteria called Bifidobacteria Infantus. (4)
The results were that the good bacteria produced an
acid that inhibited the growth of bad bacteria. This
means that when the pH level of the infant's intestinal
area is acidic at 5.1 to 5.4 due to beneficial bacteria,
then pathogenic (bad) bacteria cannot grow.

MOTHER'S MILK AND THE IMMUNE SYSTEM

Human milk contains a variety of components that are beneficial in many ways. Unlike cow's milk, human milk proteins are easily digested, offering a great source of amino acids that help the infant grow rapidly. Additionally, some of the proteins in mother's milk are actually enzymes that digest fats and carbs and assist the infant in the absorption of calcium, iron and vitamin B-12. (5) I think that is so incredible! Mother Nature knew baby would not yet be ready for digestion and that baby's little pancreas would not secrete all the enzymes it needed, so enzymes were put right in mother's milk to help! Other proteins from mother's milk are actually antimicrobial and may provide the infant protection against pathogenic bacteria and viruses. Mother's milk contains its own antibiotics that will destroy pathogens harmful to baby without also destroying the baby's beneficial bacteria. Human milk proteins also have a prebiotic property that promotes the colonization of the intestinal gut flora. (4) Prebiotic means that organisms provide fuel to enhance the environment where good bacteria grow, much like adding fertilizer and water to grass seed. This activity creates a more acidic environment, and again, many harmful organisms simply cannot thrive in the gut in an acidic environment, but the good bacteria do.

Unique Sugar in Mother's Milk

The microbial inoculation from one generation to the next occurs when an inoculation of healthy bacteria in the infant's intestinal area is received during the birthing process and enhanced by the infant's environment and diet. Breast-feeding further inoculates the infant and maintains an acidic intestinal environment, which supports the growth of more beneficial bacteria.

Though breast milk contains oligo (few) saccharides (sugars), the name implies 'not much sugar'. In fact, the 'few' refers to sugars with low caloric value. Carliot Lebrilla, a professor of chemistry at U.C. Davis and lead author of a study published in the *Journal of Agricultural and Food Chemistry*, states that complex sugars, called oligosaccharides, are *the third most common solid component of human breast milk*, after fats and proteins. These sugars are special; they are not digested in the small intestines. They do not promote the growth of bad bacteria or yeast. One third of mother's milk is made of this special sugar and its job is to feed the good bacteria and to participate in destroying harmful pathogens. Oligosaccharides are prebiotic— they are fuel for probiotics! (6) Oligosaccharides are in neither cow's milk nor most infant formulas. The only infant formula I can find in the United States that contains prebiotics is Similac Advance Early Shield Formula. Other formulas only contain lipids (fats), proteins and of course, some supplemental vitamins. Since oligosaccharides have no nutritional value and babies can't digest them, oligosaccharides have not been present in infant formulas. In fact, research about prebiotics only began ten years ago. New research shows that 60 percent of all oligosaccharides have a specific component, called fucose, which binds to the cell walls of bacteria and participates in the destruction of harmful pathogens—further protecting the baby. What this means is that normally, pathogens or harmful organisms are "tagged" for assault and an antibody is created. Often, some part of the harmful pathogen looks like us and an autoimmune disease can develop. Oligosaccharides engulf harmful pathogens and the body destroys them without creating an antibody designed continually to attack that specific protein. The pathogen is in essence masked or hidden from the immune system. Therefore, oligosaccharides destroy harmful pathogens and "cloak" them so that the immune system will not become overactive in the process of getting rid of the foreign protein. In breast-fed infants, hypo-allergenic formulas can be used to supplement breast-feeding better *if they include oligosaccharides.* If you research prebiotics and infants, you may find that the New Zealand Food Safety Authority banned FOS in formulas in July of 2007. I find this absurd. Remember, FOS is the fruit version of oligosaccharides, called fructooligosaccharide. The statement was made that not enough research has been done to deem this additive as safe and that FOS does not occur in breast milk. This article is terribly misleading, when one third of mother's milk contains oligosaccharides! In fact, FOS has been used safely in infant formulas in the European Union since 1999.

LONGEVITY PRINCIPLE #12
Breast milk contains prebiotics called oligosaccharides that are fuel for probiotics.

For women who cannot breast-feed or choose not to breast-feed, there is some encouraging news. As discussed earlier, a sugar present in mother's milk has been shown to improve immune function but has not been shown to offer any nutritive value and therefore has not been added to infant formulas. In Europe, however, 400 pre-term and full-term infants were fed formulas containing two different kinds of oligosaccharides similar to that found in mother's milk, dairy sugars and fruit sugars. However, because these sugars do not digest in the small intestines, they add few calories. In fact, these sugars act like fiber, in that they move into the large intestine and are fermented and act as food or fuel for the good bacteria and the oligosaccharides degrade harmful organisms, further protecting baby. The results demonstrated that the prebiotic mixture stimulated the growth of beneficial bacteria such as bifidobacteria and lactobacilli and reduced the growth of harmful pathogens. (2) The good news for those who cannot breast-feed is that infants fed formula supplemented with prebiotics and probiotics show an intestinal pH that matched breast-fed babies.

OLIGOSACCHARIDES AND COLON CANCER

"As a consequence of the changed intestinal flora by the dietary or supplemented galacto-oligosaccharides (GOS) and fructooligosaccharides (FOS), the fecal pH values and the short-chain fatty acid pattern were similar to those found in breast-fed infants," said Silvia Fanaro at the University of Ferrara and collaborators in Italy, Germany and the Netherlands. (2) Short-chain fatty acids (SCFA) are the bi-product of carbohydrate metabolism by bacteria in the gut. According to Dr. John Rombeau of the University Of Pennsylvania School Of Medicine, "SCFA may play a large role in protecting against large bowel cancer." (7) FOS, GOS or oligosaccharides simply cannot be digested in the small intestines. When they move to the large intestines, they act like fiber and are fermented and act as fuel for the beneficial bacteria. SCFA is a bi-product and there is promising research that suggests the higher SCFA numbers, the lower incidence for colon cancer.

OLIGOSACCHARIDES AND ECZEMA

Further reason for adding fructooligosaccharides

(FOS) to infant formulas is outlined in a study conducted in Germany that showed, "for the first time," a beneficial effect of prebiotics on the development of atopic dermatitis (skin problems like eczema) in infants. (3) Scientists are beginning to see that oligosaccharides in mother's milk stimulate postnatal immune development by altering bowel flora, having a potential role in primary allergy prevention during infancy. Research into prebiotics is relatively new. Oligosaccharides, in essence, teach the immune system. You are among the first to hear about it!

The Gut-Associated Lymphoid Tissue (GALT) is designed to desensitize the body to harmful or foreign substances to which it is exposed. With the dramatic increase in autoimmune disease and allergy, it is evident there has been a breakdown in the GALT. Other proteins in mother's milk contain properties such as an insulin-like growth factor and epidermal growth factor that may be involved in the ongoing development of the intestinal wall and other organs. Breast milk containing oligosaccharides not only provides valuable nutrition, but also acts as a defense against harmful pathogens and aids the newborn in developing optimally.

How Long Should a Mother Nurse?

We've established that breast-feeding improves the health of the Gut-Associated Lymphoid Tissue (GALT), but how long does a mother need to breast-feed to improve the baby's GALT? A European study showed a significant decrease in infection in infants who were breast-fed for longer than 13 weeks. Breast-feeding for less than 13 weeks revealed no significant difference in health between bottle-fed and breast-fed babies. The study established that the rate of gastrointestinal infection in bottle-fed babies is significantly higher than in babies who were nursed for a minimum of 13 weeks. The study suggested that maternity leaves should be extended to at least three months to optimize the infant's health. Therefore, breast-feeding for at least three months will minimize gastrointestinal problems, however, breast-feeding for at least four months will minimize incidences of eczema, and breastfeeding for at least six months minimizes asthma. (8,9)

LONGEVITY PRINCIPLE #13
Prebiotics and Probiotics ensure an acidic
pH in the intestinal area.

✳

WHAT ABOUT FORMULA?

When formula supplements are given to breast-
fed babies during the first seven days of life, the
production of a strongly acidic environment is
delayed and the health of the intestinal wall and its
full potential may never be reached. Therefore,
even one bottle can cause harm unless it includes
supplemental oligosaccharides. Mothers who
feed formula may need to participate actively
in addressing the health of the infant's GALT
and focus on lifestyle changes and possible
supplementation. Beneficial floras are acid-loving
and require and produce an acidic environment
that *prohibits* the growth of disease causing microbes.
Bacterial presence stimulates defensive factors in
the intestinal wall that support and mature the
immune system. Under-inoculated individuals or
antibiotic-treated people have thinner intestinal
walls due to a reduction in the normal amounts
of lymphatic tissue. When inoculated with

probiotics, intestinal tissue develops rapidly, which is encouraging. (10)

Longevity Principle #14
Breast-fed babies today have an intestinal pH similar to bottle-fed babies of fifty years ago due to a reduction in the quality of inoculation from generation to generation.

Continued use of antibiotics can reduce the number of normal flora and cause susceptibility to disease by reducing the intestinal wall's defenses. Once the intestinal wall is affected, pathogenic bacteria that may have been present in small numbers are now able to thrive, move from the gastrointestinal tract to other parts of the body and participate in creating disease. Since antibiotics are one of the main contributors to destruction of probiotics, it is important to supplement with beneficial bacteria such as acidophilus and bifidus before, during and after taking antibiotics. Cultured foods containing naturally occurring probiotics include miso and certain cheeses such as camembert, brie and blue cheese. Yogurt can be a good source of beneficial bacteria provided the sugar content is low and the yogurt cultures are living. If one does not have access to mother's milk or oligosaccharides, a great source of prebiotics (food for probiotics) is fructooligosaccharides (FOS) found abundantly in tomatoes, asparagus, onions, beets and more, or FOS can be supplemented.

When the intestinal wall is immature, the gut becomes more sensitive to "invaders" leading to a hyperactive immune system, which can result in autoimmune disease. The infant acquires microbial flora (good bacteria) from its first day of life as a result of being born with a sterile gastrointestinal tract. This flora is responsible for a major part of the development of the infant's entire immune system. It is now known that imbalances in the infant's intestinal bacteria may significantly increase the risk of childhood allergy and susceptibility to infectious disease. (6, 8, 9, 11-16)

In the 1920s and 1930s, evaporated milk became

commercially available at low prices. The affordability of evaporated milk and the availability of home iceboxes initiated a tremendous rise in the use of evaporated milk formulas. By the late 1930s, the use of evaporated milk formulas in the United States surpassed all commercial formulas and by 1950, more than half of all babies in the Unites States were reared on such formulas. (17) Therefore, more than half of this population was "under inoculated," creating a higher pH level in the intestinal area that inhibits the growth of beneficial bacteria and promotes the growth of harmful bacteria.

The next generation will be subject to the initial inoculation it receives from today's women. When factoring in three generations that include a degeneration of optimal inoculations, dramatic increases in vaccines and antibiotics, high sugar diets and stress, it becomes imperative to intervene and educate mothers to the relationship between optimal health, the intestines and the immune system. It is time to teach all young women that the gut trains the immune system. It is time to tell all who suffer from hyperactive immune systems and autoimmune disease about the gut/

immune system relationship. The time for relying on drugs alone has long past. We have the ability to restore the health of the intestinal area before "Generation Next," and in so doing, improve the health of individuals today and the health of future generations.

INTESTINAL pH AND THE IMMUNE SYSTEM

The ecology of the bacteria in the intestines and the GALT change when a baby is fed formula instead of being breast-fed. Babies fed formula have higher intestinal pH level (approximately 5.9 to 7.3) with a variety of different bacteria that promote more disease causing microbes such as strep or E. coli. In infants fed a combination of breast milk and formula supplements, the average intestinal pH level was approximately 5.7 to 6.0 during the first four weeks and fell to 5.45 by the sixth week. (3) Unfortunately, when breast-fed babies are given formula supplements during the first seven days of life, the creation of a strongly acidic environment is delayed, possibly indefinitely. What this means is full maturity of the GALT may never occur. When the intestinal area is not allowed to develop, then the intestinal wall integrity may not mature.

If you suffer from chronic conditions, this may be you. Whether you are an adult or a child does not matter. We must restore the integrity of the intestinal wall and improve the health of the GALT which will strengthen our immune systems. Would you feed a newborn a bowl of chili? Of course not! You know the infant's stomach is not yet able to digest food fully. An infant's intestinal area is so premature that the baby would have a reaction to something as strong as chili, eggs or honey, yet many adults are reacting to the same foods because the integrity of their gut is similar to an infant's. The reaction that results is due to the introduction of incompletely digested proteins into the digestive tract, putrification due to improper pH, deficiencies in absorption and assimilation of vitamins due to low probiotic numbers and ultimately, an assault on the GALT! The immune system eventually identifies a protein as a foreign invader creating an antibody that "tags" the protein for continual attack.

Unfortunately, by now you know that many times the body attacks itself resulting in autoimmune disease; this happens in adults with an immature GALT. If it doesn't, the stress of these proteins and toxins on the body creates more free radicals and oxidative stress, which I discuss in detail in *forever young and vibrant*. What if adults with health challenges also have an immature intestinal area that directly affects their immune systems?

LONGEVITY PRINCIPLE #15
Baby's intestinal pH needs to stay acidic so harmful pathogens like strep, E. coli and staph cannot grow.

CELIAC DISEASE AND LOW IGA
IgA antibodies were introduced earlier as a decisive benefit to overall immune health. Beneficial bacteria influence the development of the gut IgA, which is an antibody that is part of the immune system. IgA is different from antibodies we discussed earlier. Antibodies of the immune system are designed to "tag" and attack foreign proteins found on viruses, bacteria and ingested proteins. IgA, however, is predominant in the

intestinal area and will identify a foreign protein and attack it basically one time only without creating an identifier that will continue to attack the same sequence of amino acids when it sees it. An abundance of beneficial bacteria corresponds with an abundance of IgA; the more IgA, the less potential for the immune system to overreact. A mature and properly developed intestinal area is more selective about what passes into the blood stream and IgA are the decision makers. Additionally, low IgA is linked to autoimmune disease and celiac disease. The development of the intestinal area and the maturity of the GALT increase faster in breast-fed babies than in formula fed babies. If this maturation does not happen, the intestines will become more permeable, or porous, and will allow more harmful substances to pass from the intestinal area and into the bloodstream. (19,20)

LONGEVITY PRINCIPLE #16
Probiotics set the immune
system's "thermostat."

PROBIOTICS, STREP AND OCD

More diseases and disorders are being linked to
imbalances in the ecology of the intestinal area.
For instance, some obsessive compulsive disorders
(OCD) have been linked to strep, according to Dr.
Susan Swedo of the National Institutes of Mental
Health. Strep grows readily in an infant's intestinal
tract when pH levels are overly alkaline due in part
to early feeding of formula, early introduction of
solid food or poor inoculation from mother. (21)
Remember, antibodies attack proteins. The strep
virus has surface proteins that look like the brain!
When the immune system produces antibodies to
attack the strep virus, reports show that the antibody can mistakenly attacks the brain and OCD
results. Treatment is penicillin to kill the strep.
Often, OCD is minimized with antibiotics. But
what if the increase in neurological disorders is in
part due to the present day population's increase
in harmful bacteria (pathogens) in an intestinal

area that is out of balance, allowing strep to grow? Would probiotics be more helpful than penicillin?

C-Reactive Protein and Probiotics

I could share many more research articles on the beneficial aspects of probiotics and the positive effects of a healthy intestinal area, but for the sake of your heart, probiotics lower C-reactive protein, a marker of inflammation in the arteries that can be an indicator of future cardiovascular disease. (24) forever young and vibrant includes a more thorough discussion of arterial inflammatory markers.

E. Coli and Intestinal pH

The growth of E. coli is inhibited when the intestinal area's pH level is between 4.8 and 5.6. Additionally, when the intestines' pH level remains below 5.6, beneficial bacteria such as Lactobacillus bifidus grows abundantly. Infants that are breast-fed have a low intestinal pH, low numbers of E. coli bacterium and high counts of lactobacillus bifidus. On the other hand, babies fed formula have higher intestinal pH levels, higher numbers of E. coli and low numbers of L. bifidus.

C-SECTIONS AND E. COLI

On August 22, 2008, an article appeared in the *Seattle Times* that described a sixty percent increase in C-sections in Washington State. The state increase slightly exceeded the national increase in C-sections. Evidence shows that C-section babies have more E. coli in their intestinal areas. Without an initial inoculation from mother, these children absolutely need a focus on the development of the intestinal ecology after they are born, with breast-feeding and possibly supplementation of oligosaccharides. Additionally, these children need to wait to be introduced to solid foods to ensure that a proper acidic pH level is attained in their intestinal tracts. Maybe C-section babies should have regular stool sample tests to direct mothers better on action to take after the infants are born since C-section babies have higher levels of E. coli. The stool samples could check fecal pH. If the fecal pH is overly alkaline, then mothers could be directed to supplement with more probiotics and prebiotics made specifically for infants.

LONGEVITY PRINCIPLE #17
Those who have an underveloped GALT
are prone to more allergies, asthma,
eczema and autoimmune disease.

※

ASTHMA AND INFANT INTESTINAL ECOLOGY

Whether breast-feeding offers a child any protection against developing asthma and other allergies has long been controversial in the "breast vs. bottle" debate. As I mentioned earlier in this chapter, breast-feeding for at least the first six months of the baby's life can significantly reduce a child's risk of developing allergies, eczema and childhood asthma. I repeat this information because asthma has been linked to increased exposure to viral infection while young, which makes sense, since an immature intestinal area increases the body's exposure to viruses due to low IgA levels. (1,6,8,9,11-16). "Solid foods should not be introduced until six months of age; dairy products delayed until one year of age, and the mother should consider eliminating peanuts, tree nuts, cow's milk, eggs and fish from her diet (while nursing)." (1)

LONGEVITY PRINCIPLE #18
Solid food should not be given to a baby for six months, and no cow's milk for one year.

❋

BACTERIA IN THE NEWS

The public health agency of Canada noted on October 8th, 2008 that twenty Canadians had died from meat tainted with Listeria bacterium. Health officials warned people that the incubation period for Listeriosis is seventy days and pregnant women, newborns, older people and those with compromised immune systems were at greatest risk. Can you imagine how people who ate the tainted meat felt as they had to "wait and see" the results of their exposure to the meat? Amazingly, a separate article published June 20, 2007 in the "Science Daily" reported that a probiotic that lives within humans' intestinal areas called lactobacillus salivarius "offered significant protection against Listeria by producing antibiotic-like compound called bacteriocin." (18) Would it help those who may have eaten the tainted meat to consume lactobacillus salivarius during the seventy day incubation period? Yes!

I am hoping that if the media really wants to educate (help) the public, then ads will promote improving the health of the intestinal area and supplementing with probiotics. The advertisements have to be for more than an Activia commercial, though it is a good start. A July 30, 2009 article from the *Seattle Times* noted that 120 million people are targeted for swine flu vaccinations in the fall. The target population is all pregnant women and all people ages six months to 24 years. Senior citizens are not targeted for vaccination because 'they may have picked up some immunity to the swine flu in their lifetime.' I know many people are afraid, but I promise, if more time is spent improving the internal terrain or the body, there would be less infectious disease. Once again, we need to support the health of our intestinal area, thus supporting our immune system. We need not fear disease!

HUMAN MICROBIAL ECOLOGY: ARE WE MICROBIALLY BANKRUPT?

Nigel Plummer, Ph.D., author of "Optimal

Digestion," states,

You often hear about ecology, the
relationship between organisms and their
environment. Within your body there is
an entire miniature ecosystem, a micro-ecology,
which has a major influence on your health. This
inner ecology is made up of micro flora, more
than 500 species of microscopic living bacteria,
creating an internal environment that is diverse,
complex, interrelated, and dynamic or ever
changing. This population, although seemingly
minute, is so enormous that the number of
microbial bacteria in our body at any one
time is greater than the total number of all the
other cells in our body. The micro flora is essential
to our wellbeing. These bacteria provide very real
beneficial effects. They limit the populations of
harmful bacteria. They assist in the process of
digestion. They manufacture essential nutrients.
When our gut ecology is in balance, we thrive. (25)

LONGEVITY PRINCIPLE #19
The more balanced the mother's microbial
state, the better the infant inoculation.

※

WHY DO WE NEED TO SUPPLEMENT WITH PROBIOTICS NOW?

We have been consuming probiotics for thousands of years. Only since the 1940s and the dawn of refrigeration, the birth of antibiotics, preservatives, chemicals and the decrease in breast-feeding, have we been so dramatically impacted. Prior to refrigeration, one way that society preserved foods was through fermentation. Fermented foods have been used for thousands of years, since food begins to spoil the moment it is harvested. The development of civilization would have been difficult without a way to preserve foods. Harvesting meant storing; storing meant fermenting and fermenting means probiotics.

Historically, man did not need to buy probiotics. Probiotics came from sauerkraut, relish, pickles, beer, chutney and even cheese and alcohol.

Today's food does not require the same microbes, since many foods are stored in refrigerators and use preservatives. Sugar and preservatives have replaced beneficial microbes and now we are left with a deficit that must be restored. It's too bad, as the microorganisms in the fermentation process produced vitamins, enzymes, antioxidants and phytonutrients. Today we go to the health food store to buy products that help with PMS, like phytoestrogens, or supplements that help with vision like carotenoids, or flavenoids in green tea that we hope will prevent diseases like cancer. All of these are phytonutrients, small elements that are beneficial to our health. Many of you refuse to supplement, but fail to recognize that for thousands of years, man "supplemented" with bi-products of the fermentation process.

Hidden Antibiotics

After all this talk about intestinal bacterial ecology, some of you are thinking, "Yeah, but I've never taken any antibiotics in my life." Well, unless you eat organic, farm-raised meat, dairy and eggs, you have. When our daughter, Morgan was fourteen, she was taking natural horsemanship classes at a nearby barn. We lived in a suburban neighborhood. Josh came regularly and pined over the chicken coop, begging for chickens. The barn owner told Josh he could use the coop. We went to a local farm store, and much to my surprise, springtime meant time for getting little chicks. I am a city girl and had no idea. What a mistake bringing my eleven year old son into a shop with baby chicks everywhere. I was weak and we walked out with a baker's dozen of little cute chicks. Josh and I then attended a class on raising chickens. I justified my weakness with the idea that we could have healthy eggs as a benefit.

During the class, the instructor told us that all chick feed comes with antibiotics. I was shocked. I said I didn't want feed with antibiotics since that was one of the main reasons I got the chicks. Well, I could not find chicken feed free of medicine! Who knew that for years farmers have given chickens antibiotics to protect them from disease and we have unknowingly been exposed to far more antibiotics than our doctors prescribe? In a 2004 agricultural journal report, scientists found that probiotics given to chickens protect them (and us) from salmonella and other pathogens that cause food borne illness as well, if not better, than antibiotics. (26)

When I took our baker's dozen of chicks to the barn, I found the owner had missed some payments and was closing shop. So I was left with thirteen chicks, no farm, no coop and an angry husband. We kept the chicks in our garage for thirteen weeks until I could find someone to take them. I wish you could have seen our neighbors passing by and peering in at the red light over the dog crate!

For those of you who may think this book is a suggestion to avoid all medications, nothing could be farther from the truth. When my daughter was eighteen, she had a wisdom tooth infection that abruptly appeared. Antibiotics can save lives and doctors put her on an antibiotic which was absolutely necessary. Unfortunately, within thirty days of being on the necessary antibiotic, Morgan came down with an E. coli infection in her kidneys. She was very sick. We need to emphasize the effects of medications as they relate to our microbial ecology. Since Morgan was C-section, not breast-fed, and had foods introduced far too early, her intestinal ecology was already fragile. Another round of antibiotics for the E. coli found her having allergic reactions to everything she was eating. She was vulnerable because her intestines were compromised as a youngster. She took months and months of antibiotics for sinus and ear infections, so we had to be careful. When she was done with the medication, I fed her like an infant for three months so she could digest foods and restore her intestinal ecology without suffering from asthmatic and inflammatory episodes. I applied the principles I will discuss in Chapter 14 to restore her intestinal ecology. She is well now, but I wonder what happens to children in Morgan's same situation when the parents do not understand the profound relationship between wellness and absorption? Hopefully these parents will read this book, or you will pass it along. We as a people can read books like this and then demand that warnings appear on medications that encourage users to supplement with nutrition that may be depleted by the use of the medication.

It is my mission that all doctors on the planet modify their medical protocols to include addressing the health of the intestinal area and observing intestinal pH levels, the intestinal bacterial ecology and the Gut-Associated Lymphoid Tissue.

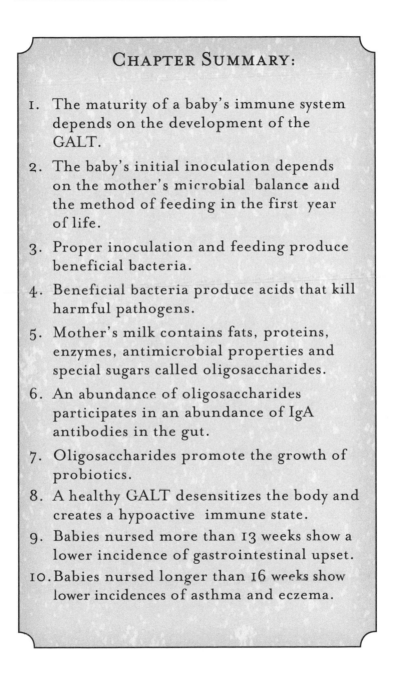

Chapter Summary:

1. The maturity of a baby's immune system depends on the development of the GALT.

2. The baby's initial inoculation depends on the mother's microbial balance and the method of feeding in the first year of life.

3. Proper inoculation and feeding produce beneficial bacteria.

4. Beneficial bacteria produce acids that kill harmful pathogens.

5. Mother's milk contains fats, proteins, enzymes, antimicrobial properties and special sugars called oligosaccharides.

6. An abundance of oligosaccharides participates in an abundance of IgA antibodies in the gut.

7. Oligosaccharides promote the growth of probiotics.

8. A healthy GALT desensitizes the body and creates a hypoactive immune state.

9. Babies nursed more than 13 weeks show a lower incidence of gastrointestinal upset.

10. Babies nursed longer than 16 weeks show lower incidences of asthma and eczema.

11. Formula (without oligosaccharides) given to infants in the first seven days of life can permanently raise intestinal pH.

12. The baby boom generation was the first generation in the history of mankind where more than 50% were taken off of breast milk (filled with oligosaccharides) and given evaporated milk.

13. Few oligosaccharides are related to few IgA antibodies.

14. Low IgA levels are found in patient with celiac disease.

15. Low IgA levels are prevalent in individuals with low probiotics in intestinal area.

16. An abundance of probiotics reduces strep in the gut.

17. Strep has been linked to obsessive compulsive disorders in children.

18. Low probiotics in the intestines creates an elevated pH.

19. An elevated pH can cause lactose intolerance.

20. Abundant probiotics in the intestinal area can lower C-reactive protein.

21. C-section babies have elevated E. coli as compared to vaginally delivered babies.

22. We need probiotic supplementation now more than ever due to the lack of preservation via fermentation, the refrigeration age and hidden antibiotics in our foods as well as an overuse of antibiotics.

DEBI'S DIALOGUE

Wouldn't it be great if organizations that promote breast-feeding such as the La Leche league, Ob/gyn's and Pediatricians discussed the inoculation of one generation to the next?

There is an opportunity to better understand the impact of not only breast-feeding, but developing and supporting a healthy intestinal microbial ecology that will ultimately support and improve the immune system and overall health.

saving 'generation next'
begins with restoring our intestinal ecology.

CHAPTER

14

Solutions

*"It is difficult to say what is impossible, for the
dream of yesterday is the hope of today and the
reality of tomorrow."*

~ ROBERT H. GODDARD

By now, you understand some of the reasons we are seeing an increase in certain diseases. The next question is, "How do we correct this?" The medical community's idea of prevention begins with immunizations and vaccinations. saving 'generation next' has established that the first inoculation comes from the mother during the birthing process and is further developed by breast-feeding and proper introduction of formula and solid foods. The first inoculation supports the maturity of the intestinal wall by improving intestinal pH and gut

IgA antibodies. The proper development of the gut directly impacts the immune system.

We now know that if the intestinal area is negatively affected, then the immune system becomes hypersensitive. So how do we address and correct this situation? How do we reduce intestinal wall inflammation and support the maturity of the intestinal wall once it is damaged?

Below is a list I created for my family as I understood the relationship between wellness and absorption. I saw what was lacking and sought to improve it. For instance, in unhealthy individuals, evidence demonstrates that low probiotics, inflammation of the intestinal wall and an immature GALT leads to increased free radical production, leading to increased oxidation. Below is a list of what I did. My goal is not to prescribe anything for you, but to stimulate a discussion in the scientific community that could offer a scientifically proven protocol to improve our intestinal inoculation and overall immune health.

Remember, brilliant scientists like J. Craig Venter have already composed the DNA of human microbes and are beginning research on their impact on our health. I have approached a company that has access to this kind of research and scientists with the ability to produce the protocol I have proposed. I look forward to sharing the good news of the results of these discussions with you at a later date. For this reason, I encourage you to take this book to your doctor. Do not try to self-prescribe. Rather, continue to gather more information on this topic. I hope you find a doctor who is participating in preventative programs and has a strong understanding of nutritional supplementation. I work with doctors who are affiliated with Nutrametrix Advanced Nutraceuticals. These doctors receive continuing education that covers nutritional research and the educational units are approved by the American Medical Association. I encourage you to find a doctor who merges allopathic (traditional) medicine with alternative (natural) medicine. Also, look for a doctor who employs a wellness consultant and if the doctor offers nutritional supplements, make sure the efficacy of the supplements are backed by clinical studies. Ask your doctor if he offers an intestinal health protocol and isotonic nutrition.

PREPARING THE SOIL—GLUTAMINE, INULIN AND ALOE

If your intestinal wall is like your front yard, how do you grow green luscious grass free of weeds and mushrooms? You prepare the soil, you spread the seed and you add fertilizer for optimum pH and you water the grass.

L-GLUTAMINE

When it was first discovered, glutamine was called the "intestinal permeability factor," because it is a nonessential, but vitally important, amino acid responsible for repairing tissue subject to rapid turnover, such as the intestinal wall. L-Glutamine is by far the most important nutrient for intestinal health. The intestinal wall very rapidly "sloughs off" tissue and rebuilds. L-Glutamine is the chief source of energy for the cells of the intestinal lining. (1) In unhealthy individuals, glutamine can also be a precursor to glutathione, a powerful antioxidant. Research shows that those who suffer from health conditions ranging from autism, diabetes even to cancer have low glutathione levels. We'll talk more about glutathione in forever young and vibrant. There are tests that check glutathione levels in the blood, and fecal tests that check the balance of beneficial bacteria to pathogens in the stool (feces). Mother's milk contains epidermal growth factor that nourishes rapidly developing tissue such as the intestinal wall. L-glutamine acts much the same way. The intestinal wall constantly "sloughs off" and rebuilds. This is a natural and healthy process and is more effective with proper nourishment.

I was inspired after reading a story by Donna Williams. If you do an internet search for Donna and autism, you will find her blog. She describes herself as being diagnosed autistic in the early 1970's. Her story is remarkable as she tells of physically collapsing with extreme intestinal and immune system challenges at the age of 24. Ultimately, Donna has recovered by improving the health of her intestinal area and thus her immune system and is one of the first autistic people to actually write about what it was like being autistic. Donna speaks about the benefit of L-glutamine. However, like many supplements, you want to be careful. A small percentage of autistic children have developed migraines taking glutamine. It seems fair to try it for 30 days and watch for symptoms. Although you may not be autistic, I am convinced that autism is an extreme imbalance in the intestinal area which creates great oxidative stress on the body. Oxidative stress depletes the body of glutathione (our built in antioxidant to rid us of toxins). Autism is the extreme of a broad spectrum of disorders, but they all originate in the gut. The metabolic pathways of glutathione, glutamine, methionine and more are far too complex for this discussion. However, the glutamine, glutathione connection is discussed in forever young and vibrant.

PREBIOTICS: INULIN, FOS AND OLIGOSACCHARIDES

Either you were not breast-fed and did not have access to the beneficial prebiotics called oligosaccharides, or you have a history of stress, high sugar and multiple medications that may have damaged your intestinal bacterial ecology. The body cannot digest oligosaccharides, but beneficial bacteria can. In the Galapagos Islands, for instance, lives a turtle that eats seaweed. The turtle is entirely unable to digest the seaweed, but probiotics in the turtle's intestinal area can. Fructooligosaccharides (FOS) and galactooligosaccharides (GOS) are supplemental oligosaccharides and are also short chains of sugar molecules, namely, fructose molecules and galactose molecules that come from glucose (found naturally in sugar beets). I used FOS because research about this special prebiotic started ten years ago. Of all oligosaccharides, FOS has been the most researched. There are other oligosaccharides, but to date, GOS, MOS and XOS have not been researched as much as FOS. FOS can be a sweetener that has half the sweetness of sugar. These sugars are not digestible in the human intestinal area, but they are fermented by the colon bacteria to act as fuel and may help destroy harmful bacteria. Research also shows that FOS may lower cholesterol and blood sugar and improve the absorption of minerals such as magnesium and calcium, improving bone density. (2,3) The best sources of FOS are Jerusalem artichokes, garlic, asparagus and onions. There is some controversy over FOS as a prebiotic since most supplemental FOS is derived from a process of bleaching cane sugar and this is not thought to be a good source. I used green powder with FOS in a smoothie shake for my children and I increased natural foods that contain FOS. Inulin is a prebiotic, similar to oligosaccharides or FOS and is found naturally in onions, leeks, or my favorite, sweet potatoes. A study done for one year with 50 teenage boys and 50 teenage girls showed a dramatic improvement in bone mineral content and bone mineral density after supplementing with inulin. "Daily consumption of a combination of prebiotic short and long-chain inulin-type fructans significantly increases calcium absorption and enhances bone mineralization during pubertal growth." (4)

ALOE VERA JUICE—ALOE

The aloe plant has been used for thousands of years to treat a myriad of health conditions. Aloe has more than 200 nutritional elements, including vitamins and minerals, enzymes, amino acids and special sugars called mucopolysaccharides. Aloe has been shown to support the immune system because the mucopolysaccharides insert themselves into our cell membranes, creating a more liquid and permeable cell membrane that better allows toxins to escape and nutrients to enter. When our cell membranes are more permeable to nutrition and better able to get rid of toxins, we are healthier. Polysaccharides seem to be naturally anti-inflammatory, anti-viral, anti-bacterial, anti-fungal and anti-parasitic. Clinical studies show that supplemental polysaccharides of 300mg/kg of body weight improves blood lipid levels in diabetics by lowering triglycerides, free fatty acids, blood sugar and improving the HDL/LDL ratios. Aloe also improved plasma insulin levels. (5) Aloe is the only known substance that improves the absorption and effectiveness of vitamins C and E. "The absorption is slower and the vitamins last longer." (6)

Aloe contains mucopolysaccharides, mother's milk contains oligosaccharides and both have similar properties. What's interesting is that humans produce mucopolysaccharides through puberty, keeping cell membranes very permeable. After puberty, humans lose this capability. I often wonder if the increased cellular permeability pre puberty is related to the ability to learn faster and be more receptive to information at a younger age? Aloe improves cellular permeability, reduces inflammation in the intestinal wall, improves intestinal peristalsis (the rhythmic contractions that move feces through the intestinal tract), is anti-viral, anti-fungal and anti-parasitic.

DIGESTIVE ENZYMES:
LIKE EARTHWORMS IN THE SOIL

Remember what Linus Pauling said—we must receive optimal concentrations of nutrients in every cell of the body. Are we doing that? Since our bodies make digestive enzymes to break down food, do we need to take additional enzymes? Absolutely yes, according to Dr. Edward Howell, author of "The Food Enzyme Concept." Supplementation with enzymes preserves our supply of enzymes in the pancreas. (7) Research shows that people who do not experience optimal wellness have low digestive enzymes. Enzymes "speed up" the metabolic process. For instance, magnesium is used in 300 enzyme processes in the body, yet a great portion of the population is low in magnesium. As discussed above, oligosaccharides improve the absorption of various nutrients including magnesium. Enzymes matter and there is a relationship between enzymes, oligosaccharides and probiotics. In the past, we ate plenty of fruits and vegetables and needed less supplemental enzymes. Today people eat more processed foods and many people take antacids, which may disrupt an enzyme's ability to digest proteins due to an altered pH level. As a result, we may want to supplement with digestive enzymes.

Research shows:

- When we eat cooked food, any possible enzymes are destroyed and our bodies must provide all of the needed enzymes.
- We were designed to eat foods such as fresh fruits and vegetables, which contain enzymes, to assist in digestion.
- Our white blood cells multiply when we eat cooked food. (8,9)
- White blood cells are used to transport digestive enzymes to digest the enzyme deficient food we eat.
- Foods such as fresh fruits and vegetables, with naturally occurring enzymes do not raise white blood cell numbers.

In other words, we stress our immune systems when we eat large amounts of enzyme deficient (cooked) food!

Pancreatic enzymes are primarily responsible for digesting food. Plant enzymes spare the pancreas and work in three ways. Plant enzymes are pre-digestive. Whole foods come with their own enzymes to ensure optimal digestion and assimilation of nutrients. When the food we eat has inadequate enzymes, then once it leaves the stomach and enters the intestinal area, the pancreas offers additional enzymes to digest the food. Therefore, we want to spare the pancreas and eat more whole foods. The pancreas was designed to provide enzymes over a lifetime to a diet that included eating many fresh fruits and vegetables. Some use the acronym S.A.D. for the Standard American Diet which includes highly processed foods, sugar, preservatives, Excitotoxins such as aspartame and MSG and 'pretend food'. If the diet does not include natural enzymes from fresh fruits and vegetables then the pancreas can become exhausted as evident by pancreatitis and even gallstones.

If you look at your teeth, it is apparent that we were not designed to eat a great deal of meat. In fact, we should consume 70 percent of our food in its original fresh, whole state. This means fresh fruit and vegetables. Produce that is cooked, heavily steamed, frozen or canned has had its enzymes destroyed. Eating raw fruits and vegetables are beneficial with one exception, cruciferous vegetables such as broccoli, cabbage, Brussels sprouts and cauliflower. If eaten raw, cruciferous vegetables contain compounds that can slow down the function of the thyroid and therefore, should be eaten lightly steamed.

What Else Do Enzymes Do?

Enzymes are naturally anti-inflammatory, blood thinning, anti-fibrotic and fight viruses.

Enzymes are Anti-inflammatory.

There are two main types of enzymes, digestive enzymes, secreted in the digestive tract and systemic enzymes, used throughout the body. You have heard that "an apple a day keeps the doctor away." This may be true for a number of reasons. It appears that when you eat enzymes between meals (an apple contains enzymes), the excess enzymes deposit into the pancreas and are then released into the body, where they degrade harmful proteins such as bacteria, viruses and fibrinogen, therefore, participating in reducing inflammation.

Enzymes are Anti-fibrotic.

In forever young and vibrant, I speak about Omega 3 and Omega 6 as beneficial fats in our diet. In summary, Omega 3 fats reduce inflammation, while Omega 6 fats increase inflammation. Both mechanisms are beneficial. Inflammation is needed for wound healing while the reduction of inflammation can participate in reducing pain and improved viscosity of the blood. The current American diet's ratio of Omega 6 to Omega 3 is 25:1. Our bodies need a ratio closer to 1:1. Therefore, our current diet participates in the inflammation felt in the body. Both Omega 3 and Omega 6 fats go through chemical processes that produce prostaglandins. Some prostaglandins are anti-inflammatory while others cause inflammation and again, the current ratio in our diet produces far too many prostaglandins that participate in inflammatory conditions.

When tissue is inflamed, prostaglandins produce a fibrous network called fibrin. Fibrin is similar to a web of scar tissue that may cleave to the arterial walls leading to atherosclerosis, or in the kidneys leading to high blood pressure, or in chronically inflamed muscles creating fibromyalgia pain. Senility can also be partly due to excess fibrin. Are you finding that you are healing more slowly? Do you have high blood pressure? Are your wounds leaving bigger and thicker scars? Are you in pain? If so, you may have excess fibrin and need supplemental enzymes.

I often joke about the difference between a baby's ear and grandmother's ear. A baby's ear is soft and pliable. Compare that to your grandmother's ear. You brush her hair and if your brush accidentally bumps her ear, it falls off! Of course I'm exaggerating—hee-hee...but we know that cartilage becomes stiffer as we age. Part of the reason is that over time, the body lays down fibrins, a non-beneficial fibrous web and as people age, the enzymes in the body that control this process, diminish. Excess fibrin is prevalent in patients with fibromyalgia, atherosclerosis, fibrocystic breast disease, decreased function of aging organs, or uterine fibroids. (10,11,12)

Enzymes, Fibrin. CRP and Homocysteine

Plant enzymes taken between meals actually eat away at this fibrous net, reducing inflammation thereby diminishing pain. Enzymes such as bromelain, papain and pancreatin travel from the gastrointestinal tract into the bloodstream and participate in breaking down toxins, fibrins and cell debris. Ultimately, systemic enzymes improve elimination via the lymphatic system and blood vessels, thus improving circulation and reducing inflammation by reducing fibrinogen.

I spoke about probiotics reducing C-reactive protein (CRP) in the previous chapter. CRP is an indicator of inflammation in the arteries. Homocysteine is another indicator of inflammation in the arterial system. forever young and vibrant presents the dangers of elevated CRP and homocysteine. Elevated homocysteine levels can develop if a person eats a great deal of red meat, is deficient in B vitamins, has an imbalance in intestinal microflora (that produce and participate in the absorption of B vitamins) or has a genetic variation that minimizes the effectiveness of B vitamins. B vitamins participate in a metabolic pathway that converts harmful homocysteine to benign methionine. Regardless, it is important to note that elevated homocysteine levels lessen the body's ability to breakdown the fibrous net called fibrin. Homocysteine is an inflammatory marker leading to atherosclerosis because homocysteine prevents the breakdown of the fibrous net that lines the arterial system. Although this is sheer speculation on my part, I believe that the diet of

African American ancestors participates in their current increased rate of stroke.

ENZYMES, AFRICAN AMERICANS AND STROKE

African Americans are twice as likely to die from stroke as are Caucasians, when comparing white males ages 45 to 54 to African American males of the same age. The National Stroke Association reports that African American men have a threefold greater risk of ischemic stroke (arterial blockage in the brain). (13) The diets of our ancestors impacts the way bodies respond to food.

Many African Americans are descendants of slaves who were brought to the United States between the seventeenth and nineteenth centuries. This is only 200 to 400 years ago. Until then, African Americans ate a diet rich in fresh fruits and vegetables. Do African Americans inherently need more fruits and vegetables than Caucasians? My ancestors are from Europe where potatoes and meat were consumed more than fresh fruits and vegetables. Without regular consumption of fresh fruits and vegetables, do African Americans suffer more from strokes because they need more of the anti-fibrotic properties that the enzymes in fresh foods provide? Over many centuries, our bodies adapt to dietary changes. However, in just a few hundred years, I speculate that African Americans need more enzymes than descendants of cultures that lived on rice and fish, or lamb and potatoes. Should African Americans supplement with enzymes from a plant or fungal source? Enzymes from plant or fungal sources work in a broader range of pH. Should African Americans eat more fresh fruits and vegetables? If it were me, I would. I would also make sure my homocysteine levels were in normal range, and if not, I would take more B vitamins.

GENETIC TESTING

There are several affordable genetic tests available for less than $1000. I encourage you to save your money and take the test. Fortunately, the test is only needed once in a lifetime because your genes do not change. If you have a variation in a gene, you will always have the variation. The discussion of genes and gene therapy is complicated however, to break it down, DNA consists of a chain of four types of nucleotide subunits that you may remember from your science books that include four letters, A, C, G, T or adenine, cytosine, guanine, and thymine. Each of the subunits is paired, guanine, cytosine and adenine, thymine. The DNA double helix looks like a ladder and each rung is capped off by one of the four letters. For normal gene expression, the subunits must be paired. Gene expression means that the specific gene will produce a protein that instructs the body. The protein is an enzyme that acts as a catalyst to promote specific metabolic functions. A specific gene for instance, will instruct the body to use folic acid to convert homocysteine to methionine. If the letters are not paired properly, then the gene that is expressed will produce a protein (enzyme) that has faulty directions. This mismatching is called a polymorphisms and the 'instruction' will be faulty. For instance, if there is a polymorphism in the MTHFR gene, then the enzyme that is produced will not 'fit' with the folic acid and the folic acid will not be able to do its job as it relates to homocysteine. The person with the MTHFR polymorphisms may take folic acid but not see an improvement in homocysteine levels and say, 'folic acid does not work for me.' They are right, but it is not the fault of the folic acid, it is their gene variation that is at fault. Luckily, if you take the gene test, you will find numerous gene polymorphisms and have better direction on what to eat and how to exercise that is most beneficial to you. Additionally, some of the gene companies offer vitamins that are tailored to work around the faulty gene expression.

IS LEAKY GUT REAL?

We've suggested that some immune challenges may be caused by digestive dysfunction and maldigestion. However, the term "leaky-gut syndrome" may be overused. "Leaky-gut" implies that sick people are sick because their intestinal walls are more permeable and let more toxins and undigested foods pass into the bloodstream, which elicits an immune response. Many doctors encounter sick people and do not see evidence of an increase in undigested proteins in their blood, so they say the assumption that leaky gut is a hypothesis for sickness is false. In fact, the GALT over-responds to proteins, viruses and other pathogens. Remember, the gut trains the immune system. Leaky gut is a condition that occur *secondary* to other conditions, such as Crohn's disease, celiac or regular use of non-steroidal anti-inflammatory medication (that increases intestinal permeability). Ideally, the gut will desensitize the body to potential pathogens.

Though leaky gut may be real, my discussion is more about an intestinal wall that is immature and does not develop optimally due to poor initial inoculation from mother, early introduction of formula or solid foods, medications, sugar or stress resulting in an altered intestinal pH, low gut IgA antibodies and few Peyer's patches. The training of the gut's immune system is then impeded. Please understand that leaky gut is the result of a disruption in the ecology of intestinal bacteria. If a baby received a poor inoculation from mother, the child is more likely to have a negative response to lactose, wheat or other offending foods. If it were me, I would remove any foods that aggravate the condition and attempt to reduce the inflammation with L-glutamine and aloe, restore intestinal ecology (a healthy mix of good and bad bacteria) with prebiotics and probiotics; ingest supplemental digestive enzymes and enzymes from fresh produce promoting the breakdown of proteins and reducing fibrin and lastly, I would supplement with nutrition that is already digested, or isotonic.

Probiotics

In 1994, the World Health Organization deemed probiotics to be the next-most important immune defense system when commonly prescribed antibiotics are rendered useless by antibiotic resistance. (14) What does the maternal inoculation offer? Probiotics. The reality is that in the past we ate fermented foods and we needed less probiotic supplementation. Now that our diet has changed and mother's intestinal ecology has been compromised by generations of over prescribed antibiotics, stress, sugar and preservatives, we need to supplement daily with probiotics. Probiotics help produce an acidic environment in the intestinal area that can prohibit unhealthy organisms from growing, help desensitize the immune system and help in the digestion and absorption of nutrition.

Probiotics are beneficial for the following conditions:

- Allergies (22,25,26,31)
- Arthritis (rheumatoid arthritis) (16,21)
- Colitis (16,17,28)

- Colon Cancer (31,34)
- Cirrhosis (studies show that probiotics may be a better prescription than antibiotics) (27)
- Eczema (23,25,30)
- High Cholesterol (probiotics remove cholesterol from bile) (10,11,36)
- H. Pylori Infection (11,20,29)
- Inflammation (14,19,21,23)
- Immune System (23-26,32)
- Irritable Bowel Syndrome (IBS) (28)
- Vaginitis (33)
- Urinary Tract Infections (33)

MICROBIAL DYSBIOSIS

Many physicians have told me that there is no such thing as an imbalance in the bacteria of the gut unless a person has Crohn's, IBS or in extreme cases such as cancer. I have witnessed fungus growing out of the nose and mouth in a cancer patient who was taking radiation and chemotherapy—that is an extreme imbalance in bacteria. Recommended daily allowances (RDA) of certain nutrients offer suggestions to prevent disease. Where are the recommendations to create *optimal* health? If absolute deficiency in vitamin C causes scurvy, what happens over long periods of time when we just don't get enough vitamin C? Nothing? I don't think so.

Looking again at optimal levels of probiotics, what happens when we don't see extreme cases, such as fungus growing out of the mouth and nose, but we have many years with a slight imbalance? Does this exist? Yes. It is called microbial (bacterial) dysbiosis (imbalance). Examples of Dysbiosis or imbalance in bacteria include:

- In the oral cavity - thrush
- In the gastrointestinal tract — affecting allergies and asthma
- Crohn's Disease, irritable bowel syndrome, colitis
- In the vaginal cavity - yeast infection
- In the toenails - toenail fungus
- On the scalp - dandruff
- On the skin - eczema

There is now substantial research to support the beneficial effects of supplementing with probiotics.

If you have an imbalance that you can see on the outside, you have an imbalance you can't see on the inside.

In chapter 13, I discussed a study in England where breast-feeding (inoculating with probiotics) decreased asthma and eczema in babies. Research shows intestinal dysbiosis or imbalance contributes to vitamin B-12 deficiency, irritable bowel syndrome, autoimmune joint diseases, colon and breast cancer, psoriasis, eczema, cystic acne and chronic fatigue. The imbalance can also lead to an over growth of Candida albicans, or yeast, which can contribute to food allergy, migraine, indigestion, gas and depression. (1-20)

LONGEVITY PRINCIPLE #20
To remain in balance, we must first become balanced.

Symptoms of Gastrointestinal Dysbiosis

Iron deficiency	Rectal itching	Indigestion, diarrhea or constipation
Systemic reactions after eating	Nausea after taking vitamins	Sense of fullness after eating
Weak, peeling or cracked fingernails	Dilated capillaries in cheeks and nose	Post adolescent acne
Bloating, belching, burning and flatulence after meals	Chronic intestinal infections, bacteria, parasites, yeast	Undigested food in stool

Great Smokies Laboratory (now Geneva Diagnostics) 13

Diseases Linked to Gastrointestinal Dysbiosis

Addison's Disease	Asthma	Celiac Disease
Chronic Auto-Immune Disprders	Dermatis Herpetiformis	Diabetes Mellitus
Eczema	Food Allergies	Gallbladder Disease
Gastric Carcinoma	Gastritis	Grave's Disease
Hepatitis	Lupus Erythematosus	Osteoporosis
Pernicous Anemia	Psoriasis	Rosacea
Thyrotoxicosis	Urticaria	Vitiligo

Great Smokies Laboratory (now Geneva Diagnostics) 13

According to Bendig H. Hanel, author of *Intestinal Flora in Health and Disease*, "In Dysbiosis, (imbalance), organisms such as bacteria, yeasts and protozoa (living organisms) *induce disease by altering the nutrition or immune response of their host.*" (Emphasis added) (14)

In other words, our bodies respond differently to the food we eat and in fact, alter our immune response when we have an imbalance of bacteria in our gut. Probiotics may influence the metabolic activity of intestinal flora and inhibit cancer potential. To maintain the balance of the intestinal micro flora, taking probiotics will improve the digestibility of fats and proteins, improve synthesis of vitamins, help in alleviating lactose intolerance caused by the inactivation of the lactase enzyme due to an elevated intestinal pH. Probiotics can inhibit the growth of 23 toxin-producing microorganisms and help regulate the pH-providing optimum enzyme activity. More importantly, probiotics can help boost the immune system and aid in preventing cancer.

We must address the reality that we have dramatically altered the flora of our gut with antibiotics in food and the environment. We now consume 148 pounds of sugar per year per person as opposed to five pounds per person, per year in the early 1900's... and we regularly *self medicate* with antacids. Therefore, it is plausible that we have created a state of microbial dysbiosis in our gastrointestinal tracts. We must restore the integrity of the intestinal wall and educate mothers to be proactive in preparing for birth and inoculation of the next generation.

Since we no longer eat many fermented foods teaming with microbes, we are not continuing our microbial inoculation. Many mothers have a diminished capacity to inoculate babies during the birthing and breast-feeding process due to three generations of overuse of medications, early introduction of formulas to infants, chemicals, preservatives, stress, sugar and our environment. To date, there has been little discussion about how to develop or maintain our microbial ecology. Until this is addressed and corrected, we need to supplement with enzymes, prebiotics and probiotics, L-glutamine and isotonic nutrition.

Restoring My Children's Health

If my daughter ate dairy, she would suffer from

terrible sinus infections and was on months of
antibiotics. Eventually, she cried to me, 'why can
other kids eat junk and are fine but I do and I
am sick?' Morgan was eleven and Josh was eight
years old. I took out an old plastic mayonnaise jar
and cleaned it out and removed the label. I then
drilled three tiny holes in the bottom and filled
it halfway with water. As the water dribbled out I
explained to my children that the jar represented
their bodies. The water represented toxins and
'bad stuff' that we all have from our diet and
environment and the holes represented our
healthy immune system getting rid of these toxins.
I then put my hand over the holes and filled the
jar to the brim with water. I explained that some
people have compromised immune systems and
are not able to get rid of toxins very well and that
others are exposed to more toxins represented by
the added water. I looked at Morgan and said,
"This is where you are right now." I then added
water until it spilled over the top and I explained
that for Morgan, one piece of pizza or one bowl of
Ice cream put her over the edge. I explained that
when the water spilled over there are symptoms
of illness. Again, I emptied the jar halfway and
added a little water and explained that when her

friends eat a little junk, the water is not spilling over, they do not get sick. I added more water, and explained however, they will all get sick eventually if they continue to eat poorly. My children seemed to understand. I then explained that all we have to do is restore their immune system and eliminate some of the junk for a while, until 'their jar was half empty' or until their bodies became healthier. I promised them that one day soon, they would be able to enjoy life's simple pleasures without becoming sick. I explained that we would all eat like a baby for a while and reprogram our immune system.

In order to restore the intestinal ecology of my children, I fed them like a newborn for months. I supplemented aloe and L-glutamine to restore the integrity of the intestinal wall. This was twelve years ago and I remember standing in the kitchen having contests of who could make the grossest face while drinking the aloe. Fortunately today, there are a lot more pleasant tasting aloes! During this time, I fed them rice and oatmeal with fruits like bananas and blueberries. I then introduced prebiotics, digestive enzymes and probiotics to begin to restore the intestinal ecology. At this time,

I added more complex grains, fruits and vegetables and I added yogurts and fermented foods to their diet. As I watched their inflammatory conditions like eczema, asthma and sinus and ear infections subside, I added supplemental isotonic nutrition in the form of a multivitamin and antioxidant and I added Omega 3. Eventually, I added fish and poultry. It was fascinating to watch my daughter who was extremely lactose intolerant, eventually enjoy a pizza or bowl of ice cream without developing a sinus infection or experiencing G.I. upset. I never gave my children a colon or liver cleanse. Though they are valuable, if we do not address the integrity of the intestinal wall first, then a liver cleanse is much like changing the carpet in a home with a leaky roof, without fixing the roof! We must fix the roof first.

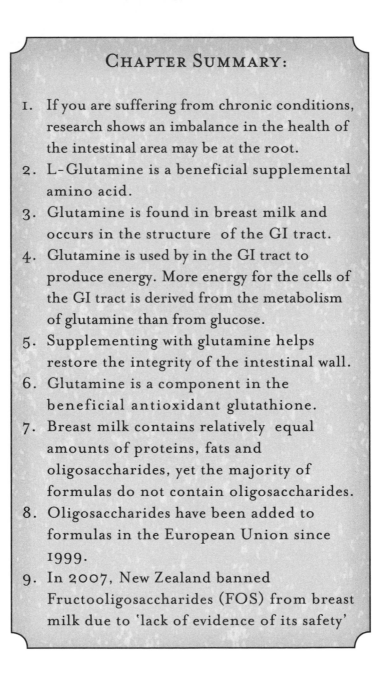

CHAPTER SUMMARY:

1. If you are suffering from chronic conditions, research shows an imbalance in the health of the intestinal area may be at the root.
2. L-Glutamine is a beneficial supplemental amino acid.
3. Glutamine is found in breast milk and occurs in the structure of the GI tract.
4. Glutamine is used by in the GI tract to produce energy. More energy for the cells of the GI tract is derived from the metabolism of glutamine than from glucose.
5. Supplementing with glutamine helps restore the integrity of the intestinal wall.
6. Glutamine is a component in the beneficial antioxidant glutathione.
7. Breast milk contains relatively equal amounts of proteins, fats and oligosaccharides, yet the majority of formulas do not contain oligosaccharides.
8. Oligosaccharides have been added to formulas in the European Union since 1999.
9. In 2007, New Zealand banned Fructooligosaccharides (FOS) from breast milk due to 'lack of evidence of its safety'

saying that FOS is not in breast milk,
when in fact, breast milk contains 1/3
oligosaccharides.

10. Supplementing with oligosaccharides,
whether GOS or FOS, may be beneficial
for raising IgA antibodies in the gut.

11. An abundance of intestinal IgA is related
to improved immune health.

12. Aloe offers natural anti-inflammatory
properties and is well documented as
a soothing tonic for the GI tract.

13. Digestive enzyme supplementation is
beneficial in the complete digestion of
proteins.

14. Enzymes from a plant or fungal source
function in a broader range of pH.

15. Enzymes are antifibrotic (fibrinogen).

16. Excess fibrin participates in fibromyalgia,
atherosclerosis, high blood pressure,
fibrocystic breast disease, uterine fibroids
or senility.

17. Plant enzymes taken between mealscan
reduce fibrins.

18. Elevated homocysteine levels diminish the
ability to break down fibrin.

19. B vitamins can reduce homocysteine levels.

20. African Americans may genetically need

more enzymes and/or fresh fruits and vegetables to reduce risk of stroke than other populations.

21. "Leaky Gut" is a misused and overused term, when in fact a more accurate statement would be, "a hyperactive immune system is related to an under developed GALT from an under developed intestinal tract."

22. Supplemental probiotics are more important now due to the reduction in natural inoculation from fermented foods with refrigeration as well as, the overuse of antibiotics and a high sugar diet.

23. When the body is out of balance, it does not act as predicted.

Debi's Dialogue

Relax.

CHAPTER

15

Thinking Positively

"Get busy living or get busy dying."

~ STEPHEN KING, *Shawshank Redemption*

A s we close this discussion of saving 'generation next' it is important to note that although individuals are responsible for their own health, government policy, pharmaceuticals, and medications have important and profound roles. I have many friends who are doctors. What I find as a common denominator in these people is a love of learning, strong curiosity, and the desire to help people. These special individuals devote more than a decade of their life learning their specialty.

However, individuals who question any aspect of the current medical model come under tremendous and often, unjustified scrutiny. One extreme example is Kevin Trudeau author of *Natural cures they don't want you to know*. I would agree that the title is inflammatory, however, I marvel at how viciously he has been attacked. In 2001, a book was released by Eric Schlosser called *Fast Food Nation* which is an incredibly critical look at a major fast food giant's gross handling of employees, animals and food. I don't recall him receiving the kinds of attacks that Kevin Trudeau has suffered. Why is it so dangerous to ask if the increase in the numbers of children's vaccinations *may be* a contributing factor to the four fold increase in chronic health conditions in children? Why is so dangerous to question staggering cancer rates when billions of dollars are spent on cancer research? Why is it so dangerous to suggest alternatives to the huge increase in pharmaceutical prescriptions that are currently written with dietary and herbal remedies? Why are individuals who suggest that Thimerosal may be a factor in autism are considered morons and out of touch? Why is it blasphemy to demand the right to buy therapeutic doses of nutritional supplementation?

I laughed the other day when in the Seattle Times, an article was released about a study conducted in Italy disproving the Thimerosal/Autism connection. The reason I laugh is because Italians do not eat the same foods as Americans. Italians do not live the same lifestyle as Americans. Autism is caused in part by extreme oxidative stress brought on by toxins, both from our diet and an immature GALT, heavy metals, diet and minimally, genetics. Yet nowhere in our society is there a platform to educate individuals on how to take care of themselves. We are trained that when we get a headache, our first question is, "Excedrin or Bayer?" Why not ask, 'what is my body telling me? Am I deficient in minerals, am I dehydrated; did I eat foods that contain excitotoxins such as aspartame or MSG? I marvel that the American Diabetic Association recommends diet coke with aspartame when aspartame has the same effects on insulin as sugar and reduces chromium which is a cofactor that drives sugar into muscle cells.

January 17, 2008, Supermodel Heidi Klum joined Diet Coke and *The Heart Truth* to help raise awareness for women about heart disease through the Diet Coke Red Dress Program. *The Heart Truth* is sponsored by the National Heart, Lung, and Blood Institute (NHLBI), which is part of the National Institute of Health. Wow, who is going to sponsor the 'Green Dress Program" educating individuals on the fact that naturally occurring OPC's reduce C-reactive protein, fiber helps reduce cholesterol levels, Omega 3's reduce inflammation, or B-vitamins reduce homocysteine levels? There is no 'Green Dress Program' because all of the aforementioned are natural and therefore cannot be patented and therefore cannot be owned and marketed exclusively. On 60 minutes, January 25th, an exciting report showed a potential new drug that may reduce cancer and prolong life called resveratrol. Why in a drug? Resveratrol comes from grape skin and is currently available through many nutritional companies. I currently take an isotonic resveratrol that has 10mg of resveratrol. It would take several bottles of wine to get the same amount! What would a resveratrol drug cost me? Would I have to wait to get a prescription to take it? Will I lose the right to buy the current resveratrol nutritional supplement?

Am I angry? No, not at all. I believe in capitalism to the core. I am a capitalist. I spent my entire adult life looking for answers for my children's health. Now people are asking me for the information I have compiled. That is appropriate. Do not get angry, get busy living and *get busy caring*. You are responsible for obtaining the information that you need to live. If you rely on the advertisements, magazines, your neighbor or even me, do not get angry if it does not work. I spend a great deal of time in my third book, the currency of thought illustrating the power of learning to hear, listen and heed your own internal voice.

Heeding your own voice requires trust. You must trust yourself and in order to do that, you must love you. I encourage you to read the first three books of my series. If you recommend one to a friend, consider where they are in their health cycle and recommend the appropriate book first.

Now is the time to take a deep breath and say, "I am in control." No matter what your current situation, whether it is poor health, relationships or finances, you are in control. When you begin to love you, and you begin to trust you, you will naturally begin to protect you.

All of us have bought into a plan. We were raised to get an education or learn a specialty and then go to work from the age of around 20 through 65 and then retire and retire comfortably. Statistics show that almost one third do not make it to retirement; they die due in large part to stress and chronic illness. Another 62% find themselves at the age of 65 relying primarily on social security. The average yearly social security compensation is $8500. Of the remaining 10%, most are still working and a very few are considered wealthy. What will your monthly social security check be at 65? Is it worth it? Considering one third die by the age of 65 and another 62% are relying primarily on social security; and only about 3% make it with incomes greater than $36,000. The question to ask is, are you part of the 3% who make it or the 97% who don't?

Dr. Klatz and Dr. Goldman, founders of the Anti-Aging Academy for Medicine (A4M) point out that the earlier you retire the longer you live. The problem is we are all so tired at the end of the day that we stop caring about 'minor' things like our health. Remember, we are a product of our habits. We are a product of good habits or bad habits, but every day we move a little closer towards happiness, wellness, peace and prosperity, or every day we move away. Change in your life will happen in small steps based on habits and consistency. Motivation comes from within. Motivation comes from having a reason why, loving, caring and passion. I cannot motivate you; I can only irritate you with knowledge. We will not make a change until the pain of our current situation is greater than the pain of making a change. We have all become a little numb. It is natural. We are exposed to a tremendous amount of information. We have become so numb and so tired that we look forward to watching others live on reality TV shows and sitcoms. We laugh with them; we cry with them, we talk about them. I think we care more about them than ourselves.

The information is overwhelming until you do one thing:

Decide what you want.

You will be amazed that the minute you clearly define what you want and focus more on what you want rather than on *what you don't want*, the information coming to you is somehow customized to answer your desires. You will no longer feel overwhelmed.

I am so happy that I did not listen or believe everything the medical community told me. If so, we would not have our son. If I had listened, my children would still be on drugs today. Instead, our son has just completed his New Cadet Basic training and has crossed the ranks to join the elite force of cadets at the United States Military Academy. Our daughter will one day have a baby that will be born through an abundantly populated birth canal and she will nurse the child and supplement and will be acutely aware of programming her child's immune system by properly developing the integrity of the intestinal area and the strength of the gut associated lymphatic tissue. Morgan was born C-section, fed cow's milk and foods far too early, and suffered years of antibiotics early on. I am certain that without intervention, she would have birthed a baby with severe reductions in the beneficial maternal inoculation and a much greater chance of chronic illness. But now, she is happy and well, what more could I ask for?

Recently, my friend went in for a free heart check.

She was told that she has A/V fibrillation and put on betablockers and Coumadin. She was advised to not eat greens, Omega 3, red wine or aspirin. She is now extremely exhausted and gaining weight. Why would she not be educated on the blood thinning effects of digestive enzymes, fruits and vegetables including spinach, Omega 3 in healthy oils and fish, one child's Bayer aspirin per day and maybe a glass of red wine with dinner? Why not check her blood after one month on that diet to see its viscosity? Be careful about believing what you are told. In the August 20, 2009 edition of the Seattle Times, an article was posted stating that we are living longer than ever. That is great, but what the article did not say is that though WE are living longer, this is the first generation where children are not expected to live as long as their parents. After watching my father die of colon cancer at 63 and my mother go from prescription drug to prescription drug, I am happy that applying the research discussed in this book with our children has in fact, saved our 'GENERATION NEXT' and hopefully yours.

Take Your T.I.M.E.

To

Improve

My

Enthusiasm

Let's break down Enthus-iasm

Enthus: God Within

iasm: I Am Sold Myself = BELIEF

To believe in you – means to trust you
– means to love YOU.

DEBI'S DIALOGUE

We the people must decide that consumers are ultimately responsible for their health.

Pharmaceutical companies must be prohibited from advertising medication on television.

School systems need to offer a comprehensive model that teaches children about the insulin cycle (discussed in forever young and vibrant) and healthy food choices.

To introduce yearly flu vaccinations, new chicken pox vaccinations or cervical cancer vaccinations without as much attention paid to caring for the body is as absurd as attempting to eliminate the mushrooms in the yard by spraying each mushroom with poison.

The way to eliminate mushrooms in the yard is to have a yard with optimal pH and nutrients and proper removal of waste, so that the environment will not elicit the growth of the mushroom spore... that is ALWAYS there.

Are you ready to take responsibility of your health?

Seven Bullet Points
Summarizing
saving 'generation next'

If you have enjoyed saving 'generation next' feel free
to recommend the book by visiting my web site,
www.justdebi.com or
info@justdebi.com

I have included a 7 point document that summarizes
the major points presented in this book; it can be
downloaded for free from my web site.   It is my hope
that this discussion happens in the grocery store line,
on the sidelines of the soccer game and eventually in
medical communities:

• *Why do so many people experience chronic health
  challenges? What is the missing link between health
  and disease?*

Do you agree that we are seeing a rise in autoimmune rates, cancer, ADHD, autism, depression,
etc.—can we blame this entirely on genetics? What
if I told you that whether you have something as
minor as allergies or as severe as cancer—many of
you have one thing in common: *an inability to digest
optimally, absorb and assimilate your nutrition?*

• *It is not so much "we are what we eat," but "we are what we absorb."*

Research shows a *profound* relationship between wellness and absorption. I'm saying that if you're not experiencing optimal health—if you have allergies, migraines, fatigue, ADHD, arthritis— then you can guess that there is an imbalance in the health of your intestinal area. The intestinal area or "gut" trains the Gut Associated Lymphoid Tissue (GALT). The GALT makes up 70% of the immune system. The healthy intestinal area produces a healthy GALT which creates a *hyposensitive* immune system rather than a hyperactive immune system.

• *There's an ecosystem of microbes in your digestive tract - actually three pounds worth!*

These microbes have many functions, from helping prepare the immune system, to assisting in assimilating nutrition, to producing vitamins and keeping toxins from entering the blood-stream. When there is an imbalance in this microbe population, the intestinal wall fails to mature. This dramatically damages our immune system response. Beneficial intestinal antibodies are now in lower numbers thus allowing a greater immune response, greater oxidative stress and a more hyperactive immune system. Left untreated, toxins and incompletely digested proteins may enter the bloodstream and contribute to disease.

• *Why don't many doctors talk about this?*

Because they think that medically, if they temporarily create a disruption in the flora of your intestines from antibiotics or other medication, your body will *restore* itself. I mean, if you cut your finger, won't it heal eventually on its own? But the Million-Dollar Question is: *"Can the body restore the balance if it was not in balanced in the first place?"*

• *Where do these bacteria come from?*

Actually, we get the beneficial bacteria one of a few ways. It begins with being born through a healthy birth canal, with "healthy" meaning a plentiful inoculation of beneficial bacteria. This is followed by breast-feeding from a mom with a plentiful inoculation of healthy bacteria and avoidance of early introductions of formula and food to the infant. Last is a continual inoculation of bacteria from the environment, fermented food and foods that contain inulin or FOS. Unfortunately, three generations of chemicals, preservatives, and high sugar diet have disrupted mother's intestinal ecology. Additionally, many of our fruits and vegetables, which should have these living microbes, have been irradiated and altered. Beneficial microbes once provided from fruits and vegetables are killed through the irradiation process. Worst of all, we lose good bacteria in many ways—antibiotics, stress, high sugar diets, birth control, steroids, chlorine and more!

• *Genetics is a snapshot of who our parents were when they were born.*

At delivery, a mother passes on not just her genetics but a snapshot of her entire life since her birth to the baby's birth. That inheritance she gives is a "microbial inheritance." Unfortunately, many of today's mothers are microbially bankrupt and cannot pass on the beneficial bacteria needed to protect the child's health.

• *We see evidence of this imbalance all around us every day.*

Imbalances are seen in the form of *babies taking antacids*, people with ulcers, ADHD, irritable bowelsyndrome, migraines, arthritis, allergies, eczema, food intolerance, fibromyalgia, rheumatism, psoriasis, colon and breast cancer, infections, acne, PMS acne and more.

DEBI'S DIALOGUE

If there is a PROFOUND relationship between wellness and the ability to absorb optimally, then doesn't it make sense to address the health of the intestinal area?

AND

If supplementing, do so with nutrition that is, in essence, already digested - or isotonic?

Debi's 4 L's

*Longevity, Laughter,
Lifestyle and Leverage*

79 Principles

Longevity Principles 1 – 20

✸

Longevity principle #1
Gut Bacteria affect the development
of the intestinal wall.

Longevity Principle #2
Our first inoculation, or "first life," does
not come from a shot. It comes from our
mothers during the birthing process and
then from our food and environment.

Longevity Principle #3
We are being inadequately inoculated
by our mothers. Due to our culture,
mothers have less to give.

Longevity Principle #4
Genetic predispositions do
not have to dictate your future.

Longevity Principle #5
There is a profound relationship
between wellness and absorption.

Longevity Principle #6
Your current circumstances do not
need to dictate your reality or your future.

Longevity Principle #7
If you don't have optimal health,
then you are not effectively absorbing,
assimilating and utilizing your nutrition.

Longevity Principle #8
Talking about our health and our
immune system without including
the health of the intestinal area is like
arguing about what octane gas to put in the
car when the engine has a head gasket leak.

Longevity Principle #9
If there is to be change, people must
resist the fear of change and drive it.

Longevity Principle #10
The gut trains the immune system.

Longevity Principle #11
The colonization of the bacteria in the
infant's intestinal area is the dawn of
the infant's immune system.

Longevity Principle #12
Breast milk contains prebiotics called oligosaccharides that are fuel for probiotics.

Longevity Principle #13
Prebiotics and Probiotics ensure an acidic pH in the intestinal area.

Longevity Principle #14
Breast-fed babies today have an intestinal pH similar to bottle fed babies of fifty years ago due to a gradual reduction in the quality of inoculation from generation to generation.

Longevity Principle #15
Baby's intestinal pH needs to stay acidic so harmful pathogens like strep; E. coli and staph cannot grow.

Longevity Principle #16
Probiotics set the immune system's "thermostat."

Longevity Principle #17
Those who have an underdeveloped
GALT are prone to more allergies,
asthma, eczema and autoimmune disease.

Longevity Principle #18
Solid food should not be given to
a baby for six months, and
no cow's milk for one year.

Longevity Principle #19
The more balanced the mother's
microbial state, the better the infant
inoculation.

Longevity Principle #20
To remain in balance, we must
first become balanced.

LIFESTYLE PRINCIPLES 1 -21

Lifestyle Principle #1
The Consumer is ultimately
responsible for her own health.

Lifestyle Principle #2
Lowering cortisol levels may reduce
obesity, depression, precocious
(early onset) puberty and even cancer.

Lifestyle Principle #3
People who are depressed are not
deficient in anti-depressants.

Lifestyle Principle #4
Fight for the right to supplement.

Lifestyle Principle #5
The "Journal of the American Medical
Association" suggests that all Americans
should take daily nutritional supplements.

Lifestyle Principle #6
Eating foods high in Omega 3's or
supplementing with Omega 3's will
participate in reducing inflammation.

Lifestyle Principle #7
Increasing CLA and reducing other sources
of Omega 6's are beneficial for fat loss and
lowering incidences of breast cancer.

Lifestyle Principle #8
The ideal ratio of total cholesterol to
HDL is 2-3. For instance, if
total cholesterol is 180 and HDL is 60,
your ratio is 3.

Lifestyle Principle #9
Consuming 5.8 grams of trans-fat each day
raises cardiovascular disease by 53%.
LOWER TRANS-FAT INTAKE.

Lifestyle Principle #10
Trans-fats block the beneficial benefit
of Omega 3's.

Lifestyle Principle #11
Age is just a number.

Lifestyle Principle #12
Antioxidants decrease inflammation.

Lifestyle Principle #13
Nutritional supplementation is more important as we age because more free radicals and fewer antioxidants are produced.

Lifestyle Principle #14
Regular detoxification of the body is as important as changing the oil in your car.

Lifestyle Principle #15
Set a goal to consume 35 grams of fiber each day.

Lifestyle Principle #16
Supplementation with Resveratrol, Selenium, Vitamin E, and ALA can help restore levels of Glutathione.

Lifestyle Principle #17
Consuming beverages with artificial sweeteners can cause you to gain more weight than drinking sugary drinks.

Lifestyle Principle #18
Eating low-glycemic foods every
two to three hours will keep
you in the fat burning zone.

Lifestyle Principle #19
Blood sugar moves into muscle
cells. The more muscle you have,
the easier it is to lower blood sugar

Lifestyle Principle #20
Strive to maintain a salivary pH of 7.

Lifestyle Principle #21
Eat 75% foods that are alkaline and
only 25% that are acid forming—unless
you supplement heavily with minerals
and greens.

LAUGHTER PRINCIPLES 1 – 28

❋

Laughter Principle #1
A gift has no value until
you open it and receive it.

Laughter Principle #2
Sometimes even the smartest people
with the best intentions are wrong.

Laughter Principle #3
Ask yourself: "What do I choose
to believe?"

Laughter Principle #4
If you ask, it will be given.
A gift often comes when you least
expect it. Be patient and do not doubt.

Laughter Principle #5
Celebrate small miracles!

Laughter Principle #6
If you are stuck in a rut, maybe you
need to start asking different questions.

Laughter Principle #7
Sometimes the greatest truths
are the simplest.

Laughter Principle #8
Until there is awareness, we
cannot see what we do not know!

Laughter Principle #9
If you believe it to be so, it will
be so—for you.

Laughter Principle #10
What we focus on grows, so what
we talk or complain about is
what we attract.

Laughter Principle #11
Knowledge is gold; be forever a student.

Laughter Principle #12
Laughter comes more easily when you change
your perception of yourself and your world.

Laughter Principle #13
Laughter comes from finding
delight in ordinary experiences.

Laughter Principle #14
Laughter comes when you are able to
forgive yourself, and forgiveness is the
foundation of loving yourself.

Laughter Principle #15
Laughter comes more readily when
you are not striving to be perfect.
THERE IS VALUE IN IMPERFECTION.

Laughter Principle #16
Your comfort zone is not "here or
there." It is within and will go with
you everywhere.

Laughter Principle #17
Laughing easily requires trust.

Laughter Principle #18
Laughter comes easily when
we are optimistic.

Laughter Principle #19
Your inner dialogue is evident
in your words and actions.

Laughter Principle #20
Laughter comes easily when
you can recognize and celebrate your
small achievements and failures.

Laughter Principle #21
Surround yourself with
images that make you laugh.

Laughter Principle #22
Laughter comes easier when you feel
satisfaction on the progress toward
achieving your goals or your dreams.

Laughter Principle #23
Laughter comes easier when
you feel you are making a difference.

Laughter Principle #24
Laughter comes easier when you
feel admired, loved and appreciated.

Laughter Principle #25
Laughter comes easier in the marriage
when the husband continues courting
and the wife minimizes criticisms.

Laughter Principle #26
Laughter comes easier when
your love bank is full.

Laughter Principle #27
Motivation comes when the pain of
your current situation is greater
than the pain of changing it.

Laughter Principle #28
Laughter and progress come easier
when you trust yourself.

LEVERAGE PRINCIPLES 1 – 10

❋

Leverage Principle #1
100% of the money you have depends
on how you think about money,
rather than on your education, your
family or your luck.

Leverage Principle #2
Strive to work smarter
rather than harder.

Leverage Principle #3
Become a good steward of your current
possessions before asking
or wanting more.

Leverage Principle #4
Decide today whether you are
poor, middle class or wealthy;
understand it and then act on it.

Leverage Principle #5
There is great wisdom in learning
how to create multiple revenue streams.

Leverage Principle #6
When starting a business, look to
invest the least amount of time
and capital for the maximum gain.

Leverage Principle #7
Study the marketplace and position
yourself at the beginning of a trend,
rather than the end of a trend.

Leverage Principle #8
Before committing to a monthly
expense, seek to create the revenue
you need to cover your new expense.

Leverage Principle #9
Identify the income you create
and live within your means.

Leverage Principle #10
If you haven't used it in
the past year, get rid of it.

BIBLIOGRAPHY

Acknowledgements

1. Department of Health and Human Services 2000. http://www.cdc.gov/nchs/about/otheract/hpdata2010/abouthp.htm

Chapter 1

1. Andrew Schuman, M.D. (2003, February). A concise history of infant formula (twists and turns included) *Contemporary Pediatric.*
2. LeFever, Gretchen, Acrona, Andrea, and Antonuccio, David. ADHD among American Schoolchildren: Evidence of Overdiagnosis and Overuse of Medication. CSMMH. *The Scientific Review of Mental Health Practice.* Retrieved from: http://psychrights.org/Research/Digest/ADHD/Overdxrx.htm
3. Lucile Packard Children's Hospital at Stanford: A Rise in Autism. Retrieved from: www.lpch.org/clinicalSpecialtiesServies/ClinicalSpecialties/PsychiatryismQA.html
4. Children's Aching Stomachs: New Research Finds Young Children are Increasingly Using Medications to Treat Gastrointestinal Ailments. Franklin Lakes, N.J., Oct. 4/PRNewswire-FirstCall

Chapter 2

1. Retrieved from: http://www.fda.gov MedicalDevices/ProductsandMedicalProcedures/DentalProducts DentalAmalgams/default.htm
2. Mersch, John. MedicineNet.com

Chapter 3

1. Perrin, J., Bloom, S., Gortmaker, S. (2007, June) The Increase of Childhood Chronic Conditions in the United States. JAMA. 2007;297:2755-2759. Retrieved from: http://jama.ama-assn.org/cgi/content/extract/297/24/2755

2. Huffpost, D. (2008, June). The Kids Are Alright. Published in ADHD, Autism, Child Health, Infant Health, Medical & Epidemiological Studies, Medical Reporting, Vaccines. Retrieved from: http://epiwonk.com/?p=81

Chapter 4

1. National Heart Lung & Blood Institute. Retrieved from: http://www.nhlbi.nih.gov/health/dci/Diseases/pah/pah_what.html

Chapter 5

1. Latsch, Gunther. (2007, March) "Collapsing Colonies: Are GM crops killing colonies?" Speigel Online International. Retrieved from: http://www.spiegel.de/international/world/0,1518,473166,00.html

2. Science News: Hatchery Fish May Hurt Efforts To Sustain Wild Salmon Runs. *ScienceDaily* (*June 13, 2009*) — Retrieved from: http://www.sciencedaily.com/releases/2009/06/090610091224.htm

Chapter 6

1. Oskar Adolfsson, O., Nikbin Meydani, S. and

Russell, R. (2004, August). Yogurt and Gut Function. *American Journal of Clinical Nutrition.* Vol. 80, No. 2, 245-256. From the Jean Mayer USDA Human Nutrition Research Center on Aging at Tufts University, Boston.

2. Roehr, B. (2007, December). HIV and the GUT: An interview with Peter Anton. *Microbicide Quarterly.* 5, (2), 3-4. Alliance for Microbicide Development.

3. Walker, M. (2000) Supplementation of the Breast-fed Baby: Just one Bottle Won't Hurt—or Will It? Massachusetts Breast-feeding Coalition. Retrieved from: http://massbfc.org/formula/bottle.html

4. Sears, CL. (2005, October 11). A dynamic partnership: celebrating our gut flora. Anaerobe. *PubMed.* (5):247-51.

5. Biradar, S.S., Patil, B. M. & Rasal, V. P. Prebiotics For Improved Gut Health. *The Internet Journal of Nutrition and Wellness.* 2005. 2 (1).

6. Salminen, S., C. Bouley, M.C. Boutron-Ruault et al. (1998). A live microbial food ingredient that is beneficial to health. Br J Nutr 1998; 80: (suppl) S147-7171.

7. Peng, Chan Lee (2007, December) Are you Feces healthy? The condition of healthy feces and the condition of unhealthy feces in related diseases.

8. Andrew Schuman, M.D. (2003, February). A concise history of infant formula (twists and turns included) *Contemporary Pediatric.*

9. Children's Aching Stomachs: New Research Finds Young Children are Increasingly Using Medications to Treat Gastrointestinal Ailments. FRANKLIN LAKES, N.J., Oct. 4 / PRNewswire-FirstCall

Chapter 7

1. Brown, Rita Mae. (1983). *Sudden Death*. New York: Bantam Books, 1983. p. 68.

2. LeFever, Gretchen, Acrona, Andrea, and Antonuccio, David. ADHD among American Schoolchildren: Evidence of Overdiagnosis and Overuse of Medication. CSMMH. *The Scientific Review of Mental Health Practice*. Retrieved from: http://psychrights.org/Research/Digest/ADHD/Overdxrx.htm

3. Livingston, Ken. (1997, Spring). The Public Interest, 127, pp. 3-18 ©1997 by National Affairs Inc.

4. Moris, Marvin & Francine Mandel, Francine (1994, October). Foods and additives are common causes of the attention deficit hyperactive disorder in children. Annals of Allergy. Vol. 73.

5. "Public Schools. Pushing Drugs?" Gov't Money May Have Sparked Surge in Ritalin Use," Investor's Business Daily, 16 Oct. 1997

Chapter 9

1. *Encyclopaedia Britannica*. Eleventh Edition

2. K. Codell Carter and Barbara R. Carter. (1994, December). Reviews and Notes: History of Medicine: Childbed Fever: A Scientific Biography of Ignaz Semmelweiss. *Annals of Internal Medicine*. Westport, Connecticut: Greenwood Press, 1994. 12/15/94, 121 (12): 999.

3. Rosenfeld, Louis (1997). Vitamin e—vitamin. The early years of discovery. *Clinical Chemistry*. 43: 680-685.

4. Fox, Maggie (2003, August). Vitamin C

may cut passive smoking damage. *News in Science.*
Retrieved from: http: www.abc.net.au/science/
news/stories/s917746.htm

5. Murray, Michael, Pizzorno, Joseph and Pizzorno,
    Lara (September, 2005). *The Encyclopedia of Healing
    Foods.* Atria. .ISBN: 0743474023.

Chapter 10

1. Murray, Michael, Pizzorno, Joseph and Pizzorno,
    Lara (September, 2005). The Encyclopedia of
    Healing Foods. Atria.ISBN: 0743474023.
2. Hume, Ethel (1942). Bechamp or Pasteur: A Lost
    Chapter in the History of Biology
3. AP (February, 23 2004). Death Knell for Great
    Barrier Reef: Report estimates that most coral
    will die by 2050. US News/Environment.
    MSNBC.
4. http://www.jcvi.org/cms/research/projects/
    gos/overview/
5. I. Nagelkerken, K. Bucan, G.W. Smith, D.
    Harvell, K. Bonair, P. Bush, J. Garzon-Ferreira,
    L. Botero, P. Gayle, C. Heberer, C. Petrovic,
    L. Pors and P. Yoshioka. (1997). Effects of
    a Widespread Disease in Caribbean Sea Fans: II.
    Patterns of infection and tissue loss. Marine
    Ecology Progress Series. 160:255-263.
6. http://www.healthfree.com/nutritional_power_
    robbins.html

Chapter 11

1. Cunningham, John D. (1989). *Human Biology.*
    New York, NY: Harper & Row.

Chapter 12

1.   Bengmark, S. "Ecological Control of the Gastrointestinal Tract. The Role of Probiotic Flora." Gut 1998: 42:2-7

2.   Biopharmaceutics. Retrieved from: ndsu.nodak. edu/instruct/balez/teaching/bioph369/ handouts/gitrach1.pdf

3.   Campbell, Neil A. (1987). Biology. 1st Ed. Benjamin/Cummings Publ. Co, Inc. Menlo Park, CA.

4.   Goldin, B.   The Microenvironment of the Colonic Cell and Bacterial Flora. Professional Resources. Tuft University School of Medicine. Retrieved from: http://www.tummywise.com/ summitsummary1.html

5.   Savaiani, J. (1997, November). Lactose Metabolism, short-chain fatty acid, and lactate production. Dig Dis Sci. 42 (11): 2370-7.

6.   Saltzman, R., et. Al. (1999). Randomized trial of *Lactobacillus acidophilus* BG2FO4 to treat lactose intolerance. *Am J Clin Nutr* 1999;69:140–6.

7.   Savaiano, D., Jiang, T. (August, 1997) In Vitro Lactose Fermentation by Human Colonic Bacteria Is Modified by *Lactobacillus acidophilus* Supplementation.   The Journal of Nutrition Vol. 127 No. 8. pp. 1489-1495.

8.   Appel, L.J., Thomas, M.P.H., Obarzanek, E. et. al. (1997). A clinical trial of the effects of dietary patterns on blood pressure. New. Engl. J. Med. 336: 1117-1124.

9.   Meilants, H. (1990). Reflections on the Link Between Intestinal Permeability and Inflammatory Joint Disease. Clin Exp. *Rheumatology.* 8(5):523-524.

10.   Pironi, L.; et al. (1990). Relationship Between

Intestinal Permeability and Inflammatory Activity in Asymptomatic Patients with Crohn's Disease. *Dig. Dis. Sci.* 35(5): 582-588.

Chapter 13

1. Peter W. Howie, J. Stewart Forsyth, Simon A. Ogston, Ann Clark, Charles du V. Florey. (January, 1990). Positive effect of breast-feeding against infection. British Medical Journal. 300 (6716): 11(6)

2. University of Ferrara. (2006, January 8). Prebiotics can improve protective properties of infant formulas. Manage Care Law Weekly. Atlanta. p. 99.

3. Walker, M. (2000) Supplementation of the Breast-fed Baby: Just one Bottle Won't Hurt—or Will It? Massachusetts Breast-feeding Coalition. Retrieved from: http://massbfc.org/formula/bottle.html

4. Wang, X & Gibson, G.R. (1993). Effects of the in vitro fermentation of oligofructose and insulin by bacteria growing in the human large intestine. J. Appl Bacteriol. 74(4): 373-80. MRC Dunn Clinical Nutrition Centre, Cambridge, UK.

5. Lonnerdal, Bo. (2003, June). Nutritional and physiologic significance of human milk proteins. American Journal of Clinical Nutrition. 77 (i6): p1537S(7)

6. Chu, Jennifer. (2006, December 6). Perfecting the Formula: Researchers have identified compounds in breast milk that might account for its oft-discussed ability to protect against certain diseases. Technology Review. An MIT publication.

7. Cummings, J., Rombeau, J., & Sakata, T, (1995). Physiological and Clinical Aspects

of Short-Chain Fatty Acids. Cambridge University Press.

8.   G. Moro, S. Arslanoglu, B. Stahl, J. Jelinek, U. Wahn, & G. Boehm. (2006, July 27). A mixture of prebiotic oligosaccharides reduces the incidence of atopic dermatitis during the first six months of age. Published Online. Doi:101136/adc.2006.098251. Archives of Disease in Childhood 2006. 91: 814-819.

9.   Zieger R. (1999). Prevention of food allergy in infants and children. Immunology & Allergy Clinics of North America. 19(3)

10.   Catassi, C, et al. (1995). Intestinal permeability changes during the first month: effect of natural versus artificial feeding. J Pediatr Gastroenterol Nutr. 21: 383-386.

11.   Bullen, J.J. (1976). Iron-binding proteins and other factors in milk responsible for resistance to Escherichia coli. Ciba Found Symp. 42:149-169.

12.   Lonnerdal, Bo (2003, June). Nutritional and physiologic significance of human milk proteins. American Journal of Clinical Nutrition. 77(i6): p1537S(7).

13.   Catassi C, et al. (1995). Intestinal permeability changes during the first month: effect of natural versus artificial feeding. J Pediatr Gastroenterol Nutr 21: 383-386.

14.   Oddy, W.H., Holt, P.G., Sly, P.D., Read, A.W., Landau. L.I., Stanley, F.J., Kendall, G.E., Burton, P.R. (1999). Association between breast-feeding and asthma in 6 year old children: findings of a prospective birth cohort study. BMJ. 319: 815-819.

15.   Pande, H, Unwin, C, & Haheim LL. (1997). Factors associated with the duration of breast-feeding: analysis of the primary and

secondary responders to a self-completed questionnaire. Acta Paediatr. 86: 173-177.

16. Hornell, A., Aarts, C., Kylberg, E., Hofvander, Y., & Gebre-Medhin, M. (1999). Breast-feeding patterns in exclusively breast-fed infants: a longitudinal prospective study in Uppsala, Sweden. Acta Paediatr. 88: 203-211.

17. Schuman, Andrew, M.D. (2003, February 1). "Marriott, William McKim; Schoenthal, L. (1929). 'An experimental study of the use of unsweetened evaporated milk for the preparation of infant feeding formulas'." Archives of Pediatrics. 46: 135-148.

18. Corr, et al. (2007, May 1). Bacteriocin production as a mechanism for the anti-infective activity of Lactobacillus salivarius. UCC 118. Proceeding National Academy Science. 104 (18): 7617-7621

19. Isolauri, Erika, Sutas, Yeldä, Kankaanpää, Pasi Arvilommi, Heiddi & Salminen, Seppo. (2001, February). Probiotics: effects on immunity. American Journal of Clinical Nutrition. 73 (2): 444S-450s.

20. Murray, I.A., Smith, J.A., Coupland, K., Ansell, I.D., & Long, R.G. (2005, December). Intestinal disaccharidase deficiency without villous atrophy may represent early celiac disease. Am J Gastroenterol. 100 (12): 2784-8.

21. Swedo, S. Leonard, H.L., Garvey, M. & et al. (1998). Pediatric autoimmune neuropsychiatric disorders associated with streptococcal infection. clinical descriptions of the first 50 cases. Am J Psychiatry. 155: 264-271.

22. Kekkonen, R.A., Lummela, N., Karjalainen, H., Latvala, S., Tynkkynen, S., Järvenpää, S., Kautiainen, H., Julkunen, I., Vapaatalo,

H., Korpela, R. (2008). Probiotic intervention has strain-specific anti-inflammatory effects in healthy adults. World J Gastroenterol. 14 (13): 2029-2036.

23. Nigel Plummer, Ph.D., "Friendly Flora" (from the book *Optimal Digestion,* chapter five, page 46.)

24. (2004, January 19). Friendly Flora: Science investigates probiotics in poultry, Develops new tests. Science Daily.

Chapter 14

1. Greenwell, Ivy. (1999, September). Glutamine: The essential "Non-Essential" Amino Acid. *Life Extension.*

2. Molis, C., Flourie, B., Ouarne, F. et al. (1996). Digestion, excretion, and Energy value of fructooligosaccharides in healthy humans. *Am J Clin Nutr.* 64: 324-8.

3. Van Den Heuvel, E.G., Muys, T., Van Dokkum, W., Schaafsma, G. (1999). Oligofructose stimulates calcium absorption in adolescents. *Am J Clin Nutr.* 69: 544-8.

4. Barkley, L., & Lie, D. (2005, August). Inulin-Type Fructans May Enhance Calcium Absorption in Adolescents. Am J Clin Nutr. 82: 471-476.

5. Beneficial effects of aloe vera leaf gel extract on lipid profile status in rats with streptozotocin diabetes.: Clin Exp Pharmacol Physiol. 2006 Mar;33(3):232-7.

6. Effect of Aloe vera preparations on the human bioavailability of vitamins C and E.: Phytomedicine. 2005 Nov;12(10):760-5. Vinson JA, Al Kharrat H, Andreoli L. Department of Chemistry, University of Scranton, Scranton, PA, 18510 4626, USA. vinson@scranton.edu

7. Howell, E. (1940). Enzyme Starvation. *The Journal of the American Association for Medico Physical Research.*

8. Kouchakoff, P. (1930). The Influence of Food on the Blood Formula of Man. First International Congress of Microbiology, Paris.

8. Ahmed, A. J. (2002). The Cycle of Life: Circulation and the Lymphatic System. Manuscript in Preparation.

10. Fuster, V. (1999). The Vulnerable Plaque: Understanding, Identification and Modification. Armonk, NY: Futura Publishing.

11. Sumi, H., Hamada, H., Nakanishi, K. and Hiratani, H. (1994). "Enhancement of the Fibrinolytic Activity in Plasma by Oral Administration of Nattokinase: Natto VR 501." *Acta Haematologica.* 84: 139.

12. www.stroke.com

13. Bengmark S. (2000). Colonic food: pre and probiotics. *Am J Gastroenterol.* 95: S5-S7.

14. Great Smokey Diagnostic Labs now known as Geneva Diagnostics.

15. Hanel H, Bendig, J. (1975). Intestinal flora in health and disease. *Progress in Food and Nutr Sci.* 1 (1): 21-64.

16. Vanderhoof, J.A. (2001). Probiotics: future directions. *Am J Clin Nutr.* 73: 1152S-1155S.

17. Drisko, J., Giles, C., and Bischoff, B. (2003, May). Probiotics in health maintenance and disease prevention-Probiotics. *Alternative Medicine Review.*

18. Madsen, K.I., Doyle, J.S., Jewell, L.D., et al. (1999). Lactobacillus species prevents colitis in interleukin 10 genedeficient mice. *Gastroenterology.* 116: 1107-1114.

19. Marteau, P.R., de Vrese, M., Cellier, C.J.,

Schrezenmeir, J. (2001). Protection from gastrointestinal diseases with the use of probiotics. *Am J Clin Nutr.* 73: 430S-436S.

20.   Aiba, Y. Suzuki, N. Kabir, A.M., et al. (1998). Lactic acid-mediated suppression of *Helicobacter pylori* by the oral administration of *Lactobacillus salivarius* as a probiotic in a gnotobiotic murine model. *Am J Gastroenterol.* 93: 2097-2101.

21.   Malin M., Verronen, P., Korhonen, H. et al. (1997). Dietary therapy with Lactobacillus GG, bovine colostrums or bovine immune colostrums in patients with juvenile chronic arthritis: evaluation of effect of gut defense mechanisms. *Inflammopharmacology.* 5: 219- 236.

22.   Murch, S.H. (2001). Toll of allergy reduced by probiotics. *Lancet.* 357: 1057-1059.

23.   Pelto, L., Isolauri, E., Lilius, E.M., et al. (1998). Probiotic bacteria down regulate the milk-induced inflammatory response in milk-hypersensitive subjects but have an immunostimulatory effect in healthy subjects. *Clin Exp Allergy.* 28: 1474-1479.

24.   Pessi, T. Sutas, Y., Marttinen, A., Isolauri, E. (1998). Probiotics reinforce mucosal degradation of antigens in rats: implications for therapeutic use of probiotics. *J Nutr.* 128: 2313-2318.

25.   Pessi, T., Sutas, Y., Hurme, M., & Isolauri, E. (2000). Interleukin-10 generation in atopic children following oral *Lactobacillus rhamnosus* GG. *Clin Exp Allergy.* 30: 1804-1808.

26.   Cunningham-Rundles, S. Ahrne, S., Bengmark, S., et al. (2000). Probiotics and immune response. *Am J Gastroenterol.* 95: S22-S25.

27.   De Santis, A., Famularo, G., De Simone, C.

(2000). Probiotics for the hemodynamic alterations of patients with liver cirrhosis. *Am J Gastroenterol.* 95: 323-324.

28. Schultz, M. & Sartor, R.B. (2000). Probiotics and inflammatory bowel diseases. *Am J Gastroenterol.* 95: S19-S21.

29. Bazzoli, F., Zagari, R.M., Fossi, S. et al. (1992). *In vivo Helicobacter pylori clearance failure with Lactobacillus acidophilus. Gastroenterology. 102: A38.*

30. Jackson, P.G. et al. (1981). Intestinal permeability in patients with eczema and food allergy. *Lancet.* 1: 1285-1286.

31. The metabolism of the intestinal microflora and its relationship to dietary fat, colon and breast cancer. (1986). *Prog. Clin. Biol. Res.* 222: 655-85.

32. Majamaa, H., Isolauri, E. (1997). Probiotics: a novel approach in the management of food allergy. *Allergy Clin Immunol.* 99: 179-185.

33. Cadieux, P., Burton, J., Gardiner, G., et al. (2002). Lactobacillus strains and vaginal ecology. *JAMA.* 287: 1940-41.

34. Moore, W.E., Moore, L.H. (1995). Intestinal floras of populations that have a high risk of colon cancer. *Appl Environ Microbiol.* 61: 3202-3207.

35. Sanders, M.E., Klaenhammer, T.R. (2001). Invited review: the scientific basis of *Lactobacillus acidophilus* NCFM functionality as a probiotic. *J Dairy Sci.* 84: 319-331.

36. No authors listed. (2002). Lactobacillus sporogenes monograph. *Altern Med Rev.* 7: 340-342.

Seven Bulletpoints

1. Jackson, P.G. et al. (1981). Intestinal permeability

in patients with eczema and food allergy. *Lancet.* 1: 1285-1286.

2.   Yates, V.M., Watikinson, G., Kelman, A. (1982). Further evidence for an association between psoriasis, Crohn's disease and ulcerative colitis. *Brit. J Dermat.* 106: 323-330.

3.   Bjarnson, I., Williams, P., So, A. et al. (1984). Intestinal Permeability and inflammation in patients with Rheumatoid Arthritis; effects of non-steroidal anti-inflammatory drugs. *Lancet.* ii: 711-4.

4.   Rowe, A.J. (1930). Allergic toxemia and migraine due to food allergy. *Calif West Med.* 33: 785.

5.   Randolph, T.G. (1947). Allergy as a Causative factor in fatigue, irritability, and behavior problems in children. *Pediat.* 31: 560.

6.   Berg, R. (1983). "Translocation of indigenous bacteria from the intestinal tract." Human Intestinal Microflora in Health and Disease. Shreveport, L.A: Academic Press. p. 333-352.

7.   Garner, M.L.G. (1988). Gastrointestinal absorption of intact proteins. *Ann Rev Nutr.* 8: 329-350.

8.   Washaw, A.L. et al. (1974). Protein uptake by the intestine: Evidence for absorption of intact macromolecules. *Gastroenterology.* 66: 987-992.

9.   Bettelheim, K.A., Breardon, A., Faiers, M.C., O'Farrell, S.M. (1974). The origin of O serotypes of *Escherichia coli* in babies after normal delivery. *J Hyg* (London). 72: 67–70.

10.   Brook, I., Barett, C., Brinkman, C., Martin, W., Finegold, S. (1979). Aerobic and anaerobic bacterial flora of the maternal cervix and newborn gastric fluid and conjunctiva: a prospective study. *Pediatrics.* 63: 451–5.

11.   Lennox-King, S.M.J., O'Farrell, S.M.,

Bettelheim K.A., & Shooter, R.A. (1976). Colonization of caesarean section babies by *Escherichia coli. Infection.* 4: 134–8.

12. Lennox-King, S.M.J., O'Farrell, S.M, Bettelheim, K.A., & Shooter, R.A. (1976). *Escherichia coli* isolated from babies delivered by caesarian section and their environment. *Infection.* 4: 139–45.

13. Mata, I.J., & Urrutia, J.J. (1971). Intestinal colonization of breast-fed children in a rural area of low socioeconomic level. *Acad Sci.* 176: 93–108.

14. Finegold, S.M., Attebery, H.R., & Sutter, V.L. (1974). Effect of diet on human fecal flora: comparison of Japanese and American diets. *Am J Clin Nutr.* 27: 1456–69.

15. Michals, K. and Matalon, R. (1985). Phenylalanine metabolites, attention span and hyperactivity. *Am J Clin Nutr.* 42(2): 361-5.

16. Birdsall, T.C. (1989, June). Campylobacter pylori and its association with duodenal and gastric ulcers. Applied Clinical Nutrition Seminar. Seattle, WA. Presentation.

17. Moore, W.E.C., Holdeman, L.V. (1975). Discussion of current bacteriological investigations of the relationships between intestinal flora, diet and colon cancer. *Cancer Res.* 35: 3418-3420.

18. Gorard, D.A., Gomborone, J.E., Libby, G.W., Farthing, M.J.G. (1996). Intestinal transit in anxiety and depression. *Gut.* 39: 551-555.

19. The metabolism of the intestinal microflora and its relationship to dietary fat, colon and breast cancer. (1986). *Prog Clin Biol Res.* 222: 655-85.

20. Henel, H. Bendig, J. (1975). Intestinal flora in Health and Disease. *Prog Food Nutr Sci.* 1: 21-64.

Glossary

A

Absorbing: To take (something) in through or as through pores or interstices.

Acid Reflux: A burning sensation in the stomach, typically extending toward the esophagus and sometimes associated with the eructation of an acid fluid.

Allergies: An abnormal reaction of the body to a previously encountered allergen introduced by inhalation, ingestion, injection, or skin contact, often manifested by itchy eyes, runny nose, wheezing, skin rash, or diarrhea.

Allopathic: The method of treating disease by the use of agents that produce effects different from those of the disease treated.

Allopathic medicine: Modern medicine, as opposed to homeopathic medicine.

Alzheimer's disease: A progressive, degenerative brain disease that affects thinking, behavior, and memory.

Amalgam fillings: An alloy of mercury with another metal (usually silver) used by dentists to fill cavities in teeth; except for iron and platinum all metals dissolve in mercury and chemists refer to the resulting mercury mixtures as amalgams.

Amenorrhea: Abnormal suppression or absence of menstruation.

Amino acid: Any of a class of organic compounds that contains at least one amino group, $-NH_2$, and one carboxyl group, $-COOH$: the alpha-amino acids, $RCH(NH_2)COOH$, are the building blocks from which proteins are constructed.

Amniotic fluid: The watery fluid in the amnion, in which the embryo is suspended.

Amylase: Any of a widely distributed class of enzymes that catalyze the hydrolysis of starch, glycogen, and related polysaccharides to oligosaccharides, maltose, or glucose.

Antacids: Counteracting or neutralizing acidity, especially of the stomach.

Anti-fibrotic: Substances that reduce fibrinogen.

Antibiotic: Any of a large group of chemical substances, as penicillin or streptomycin, produced by various microorganisms and fungi, having the capacity in dilute solutions to inhibit the growth of or to destroy bacteria and other microorganisms, used chiefly in the treatment of infectious diseases.

Antibody: Any of numerous Y-shaped protein molecules produced by B cells as a primary immune defense, each molecule and its clones having a unique binding site that can combine with the complementary site of a foreign antigen, as on a virus or bacterium, thereby disabling the antigen and signaling other immune defenses. Abbreviation: Ab

Antigen: Any substance that can stimulate the production of antibodies and combine specifically with them.

Archea bacteria: A group of microorganisms, including the methanogens and certain halophiles and thermoacidophiles, that have RNA sequences, coenzymes, and a cell wall composition that are different from all other organisms: considered to be an ancient form of life that evolved separately from the bacteria and blue-green algae and sometimes classified as a kingdom.

Aspartame: A white, crystalline, odorless, slightly water-soluble noncarbohydrate powder, $C_{14}H_{18}N_2O_5$, synthesized from amino acids, that is 150–200 times as sweet as sugar: used as a low-calorie sugar substitute in soft drinks, table sweeteners, and other food products.

Assimilate: To convert (food) to substances suitable for incorporation into the body and its tissues.

Asthma: A paroxysmal, often allergic disorder of respiration, characterized by bronchospasm, wheezing, and difficulty in expiration, often accompanied by coughing and a feeling of constriction in the chest.

Attention Deficit Disorder (ADD): A condition, usually in children, marked by inattentiveness, dreaminess, and passivity.

Attention Deficit Hyperactive Disorder (ADHD): A condition, usually in children, characterized by inattention, hyperactivity, and impulsiveness.

Autism: A pervasive developmental disorder of children, characterized by impaired communication, excessive rigidity, and emotional detachment.

Autoimmune disease: A disease resulting from a

disordered immune reaction in which antibodies are produced against one's own tissues, as systemic lupus erythematosus or rheumatoid arthritis.

B

B-6: The active form of B-6 is Pyridoxalphosphate (PLP) which is made up of three organic compounds, pyridoxine, pyridoxal, and pyridoxamine A pyridine derivative, $C18H11NO3$, occurring especially in cereals, yeast, liver, and fish and serving as a coenzyme in amino acid synthesis.

B-12: Cobalamina deep-red crystalline, water-soluble solid, $C63H88N14O14PCo$, obtained from liver, milk, eggs, fish, oysters, and clams: a deficiency causes pernicious anemia and disorders of the nervous system.

Bacteria: Ubiquitous one-celled organisms, spherical, spiral, or rod-shaped and appearing singly or in chains, comprising the Schizomycota, a phylum of the kingdom Monera (in some classification systems the plant class Schizomycetes), various species of which are involved in fermentation, putrefaction, infectious diseases, or nitrogen fixation.

Beta Waves: A pattern of high-frequency brain waves

(beta waves) observed in normal persons upon sensory stimulation, especially with light, or when they are engaging in purposeful mental activity.

Betain: A colorless, crystalline, water-soluble, sweet-tasting alkaloid, $C_5H_{11}NO_2$, usually obtained from sugar beets or synthesized from glycine, used chiefly in medicine.

Bifidobacteria: A genus of anaerobic bacteria that makes up the gut flora, the bacteria that reside in the colon.

Bile: A bitter, alkaline, yellow or greenish liquid, secreted by the liver that aids in absorption and digestion, especially of fats.

Bilirubin: A reddish bile pigment, $C_{33}H_{36}O_6N_4$, results from the degradation of heme by reticuloendothelial cells in the liver: a high level in the blood produces the yellow skin symptomatic of jaundice.

Bolus: A round mass of medicinal material, larger than an ordinary pill. Abbreviation: bol.

C

C-section: The delivery of a fetus by surgical incision through the abdominal wall and uterus.

Carotenoids: Any of a class of yellow to red pigments found especially in plants, algae, and photosynthetic bacteria. Carotenoids generally consist of conjoined units of Carotenoids, are nutritionally important for many animals, giving flamingoes their color, for example, and also have antioxidant properties. There are many types of Carotenoids, including carotenes and xanthophylls.

Catheter: A flexible or rigid hollow tube employed to drain fluids from body cavities or to distend body passages, especially one for passing into the bladder through the urethra to draw off urine or into the heart through a leg vein or arm vein for diagnostic examination.

Catheterized: To introduce a catheter into.

Celiac Disease: A hereditary digestive disorder involving intolerance to gluten, usually occurring in young children, characterized by marked abdominal distention, malnutrition, wasting, and the passage of large, fatty, malodorous stool.

Cerebrovascular disease: A group of brain dysfunctions related to disease of blood vessels supplying the brain.

Cholesterol: A sterol, $C_{27}H_{46}O$, that occurs in all animal tissues, especially in the brain, spinal cord, and adipose tissue, functions chiefly as a protective agent in the skin and myelin sheaths of nerve cells, a detoxifier in the bloodstream, and as a precursor of many steroids: deposits of cholesterol form in certain pathological conditions, as gallstones and atherosclerotic plaques.

Chromium: A co-factor that drives insulin into muscle cells.

Chronic Acid Reflux: A burning sensation in the stomach, typically extending toward the esophagus and sometimes associated with the eructation of an acid fluid.

Chronic fatigue: Widespread muscle & joint pain, cognitive difficulties, chronic, often severe mental and physical exhaustion.

CoQ10: A benzoquinone, where Q refers to the quinone chemical group and 10 refers to the isoprenyl chemical subunits.

Colitis: Inflammation of the colon.

Colon: The part of the large intestine extending from the cecum to the rectum.

Crohn's disease: A chronic inflammatory bowel disease that causes scarring and thickening of the intestinal walls and frequently leads to obstruction.

Cruciferous: Of, pertaining to, or resembling, a family of plants which have four petals arranged like the arms of a cross, as the mustard, radish, turnip, etc.

D

Dexamphetamine: A psycho stimulant that increases wakefulness and counteracts fatigue.

Diabetes: A disorder of carbohydrate metabolism, usually occurring in genetically predisposed individuals, characterized by inadequate production or utilization of insulin and resulting in excessive amounts of glucose in the blood and urine, excessive thirst, weight loss, and in some cases progressive destruction of small blood vessels leading to such complications as infections and gangrene of the limbs or blindness.

Digestive enzymes: Enzymes that break down polymeric macromolecules into their smaller building blocks.

Duodenal: The beginning portion of the small intestine, starting at the lower end of the stomach and extending to the jejunum.

Duodenum: The first portion of the small intestine, from the stomach to the jejunum.

Dysbiosis: The condition of having microbial imbalances on or within the body.

E

E. coli: A bacillus (Escherichia coli) normally found in the human gastrointestinal tract and existing as numerous strains, some of which are responsible for diarrheal diseases. Other strains have been used experimentally in molecular biology.

Eczema: An inflammatory condition of the skin attended with itching and the exudation of serious matter.

Emulsification: To make into or form an emulsion.

Enzyme: Any of various proteins, as pepsin, originating from living cells and capable of producing certain chemical changes in organic substances by catalytic action, as in digestion.

Esophagus: A muscular passage connecting the mouth or pharynx with the stomach in invertebrate and vertebrate animals; gullet.

Ethyl mercury: A cation composed of an ethyl group and a mercury atom.

Evolve: To come forth gradually into being; develop; undergo evolution.

Exocrine glands: Glands that secrete their products (enzymes) into ducts (duct glands).

Extracellular: Outside a cell or cells.

F

Fat-soluble: Soluble in oils or fats.

Federal Drug Association (FDA): Organization that regulates foods and drugs in the Unites States representing $0.25 for every $1.00 spent by consumers.

Fiber: The structural part of plants and plant products that consists of carbohydrates, as cellulose and pectin, that are wholly or partially indigestible and when eaten stimulate peristalsis in the intestine.

Fibrinogen: A globulin occurring in blood and yielding fibrin in blood coagulation.

Fibromyalgia: A syndrome characterized by chronic pain in the muscles and soft tissues surrounding joints, fatigue, and tenderness at specific sites in the body.

Flora: The aggregate of bacteria, fungi, and other microorganisms normally occurring on or in the bodies of humans and other animals.

Folic acid: A water-soluble vitamin that is converted to a coenzyme essential to purine and thymine biosynthesis: deficiency causes a form of anemia.

Food intolerances: Abnormal sensitivity or allergy to a food.

Free Radical: An atom or molecule that bears an unpaired electron and is extremely reactive, capable of engaging in rapid chain reactions that destabilize other molecules and generate many more free radicals:

in the body, deactivated by antioxidants, uric acid, and certain enzyme activities.

Fructo-oligosaccharides: A class of oligosaccharides used as an artificial or alternative sweetener.

Fungus: Any of a diverse group of eukaryotic single-celled or multinucleate organisms that live by decomposing and absorbing the organic material in which they grow, comprising the mushrooms, molds, mildews, smuts, rusts, and yeasts, and classified in the kingdom Fungi or, in some classification systems, in the division Fungi (Thallophyta) of the kingdom Plantae.

G

Gastric glands: Secretory glands in the stomach.

Gastritis: Inflammation of the stomach, especially of its mucous membrane.

Gastro-intestinal tract: The digestive tract (also known as the alimentary canal) is the system of organs within multicellular animals that takes in food, digests it to extract energy and nutrients, and expels the remaining waste.

Glutamic acid: An amino acid, HOOCCH2CH2CH(NH2)COOH, obtained by hydrolysis from wheat gluten and sugar-beet residues, used commercially chiefly in the form of its sodium salt to intensify the flavor of meat or other food.

Glutamine: A crystalline amino acid, HOOCCH(NH2)CH2CH2CONH2, related to glutamic acid.

Glutathione: A crystalline, water-soluble peptide of glutamic acid, cysteine, and glycine, C10H17N3O6S, found in blood and in animal and plant tissues, and important in tissue oxidations and in the activation of some enzymes.

Goiter: An enlargement of the thyroid gland on the front and sides of the neck, usually symptomatic of abnormal thyroid secretion, especially hypothyroidism due to a lack of iodine in the diet.

Graves' disease: A disease characterized by an enlarged thyroid, a rapid pulse, and increased basal metabolism due to excessive thyroid secretion; exophthalmic goiter.

Gut-Associated Lymphoid Tissue (GALT): The digestive tract's immune system is often referred to as gut-associated lymphoid tissue (GALT) and works to protect the body from invasion. GALT is an example of mucosa-associated lymphoid tissue. About 70% of the body's immune system is found in the digestive tract. The GALT is made up of several types of lymphoid tissue that produce and store immune cells that carry out attacks and defend against pathogens.

H

H. Pylori Infection: The type species of genus Helicobacter; produces urease and is associated with several gastro duodenal diseases (including gastritis and gastric ulcers and duodenal ulcers and other peptic ulcers).

Hepatitis: Inflammation of the liver.

High blood pressure: Elevation of the arterial blood pressure or a condition resulting from it; hypertension.

Histamine: A histidine-derived amine compound that is released mainly by damaged mast cells in allergic reactions, causing dilation and permeability of blood vessels and lowering blood pressure.

HIV: Human immunodeficiency virus. A type of

retrovirus that can lead to Acquired Immunodeficiency Syndrome (AIDS) where the immune system fails leading to opportunistic infections.

Homeopathic: Of, pertaining to, or according to the principles of homeopathy.

Homocysteine: An amino acid used normally by the body in cellular metabolism and the manufacture of proteins. Elevated concentrations in the blood are thought to increase the risk for heart disease by damaging the lining of blood vessels and enhancing blood clotting.

Hydrochloric acid: A colorless or faintly yellow, corrosive, fuming liquid, HCL, used chiefly in chemical and industrial processes, secreted by the stomach in the digestion of proteins.

Hydrogen: A colorless, odorless, flammable gas that combines chemically with oxygen to form water.

Hydrogenated Fat: A bland white semisolid saturated fat made from unsaturated liquid oil.

I

Immunologist: The branch of science dealing with

the components of the immune system, immunity from disease, the immune response, and immunologic techniques of analysis.

Indigestion: Uncomfortable inability or difficulty in digesting food; dyspepsia.

Inflammation: Redness, swelling, pain, tenderness, heat, and disturbed function of an area of the body, especially as a reaction of tissues to injurious agents.

Inoculation: The act or process of inoculating.

Insulin: A polypeptide hormone, produced by the beta cells of the islets of Langerhans of the pancreas that regulates the metabolism of glucose and other nutrients.

Insulin cycle: The relationship between food and insulin. Foods have varying glycemic indices and accordingly, insulin is released. Ideally, foods consumed are low-glycemic and will result in a slow release of insulin and therefore, a slow introduction of sugar in the muscle cells, maintaining blood sugar levels.

Irradiated: To treat by exposure to radiation, as of ultraviolet light.

Irritable Bowel Syndrome: A disorder of the intestines characterized by belly pain, diarrhea, cramps or constipation. It is not the same as inflammatory bowel disease.

Isotonic: Noting or pertaining to a solution containing the same salt concentration as mammalian blood.

L

Lactase: An enzyme capable of hydrolyzing lactose into glucose and galactose.

Lactobacillus salivarius: A probiotic that occurs in the human intestinal tract that is known to destroy Listeria.

Lactose: Disaccharide, $C_{12}H_{22}O_{11}$, present in milk that upon hydrolysis yields glucose and galactose.

Lactose intolerant: Unable to digest lactose (milk sugar) due to a deficiency of lactase, an enzyme for metabolizing lactose, unable to digest milk and some dairy products.

Large Intestines: The large intestine extends from the end of the ileum to the anus.

Leukemia: Any of several cancers of the bone marrow that prevent the normal manufacture of red and white blood cells and platelets, resulting in anemia, increased susceptibility to infection, and impaired blood clotting.

Lipase: Any of a class of enzymes that break down fats, produced by the liver, pancreas, and other digestive organs or by certain plants.

Listeria: Any of several rod-shaped, aerobic, parasitic bacteria of the genus Listeria, pathogenic for humans.

Lupus: A rare form of tuberculosis of the skin, characterized by brownish tubercles that often heal slowly and leave scars.

Lymph Nodes: Small, rounded structures along the small vessels of the lymphatic system that produce disease-fighting white blood cells and filter out harmful microorganisms and toxins from the lymph. Lymph nodes may become enlarged when they are actively fighting infection.

Lymphatic System: The system by which lymph is returned from the cells to the blood and by which white blood cells are produced in response to inflammation or presence of antigens; in mammals, the system includes the lymph glands, vessels and sinuses.

Lysine: A crystalline, basic, amino acid, $H_2N(CH_2)_4CH(NH_2)COOH$, produced chiefly from many proteins by hydrolysis, essential in the nutrition of humans and animals.

M

MRI machine: Also called NMR. Magnetic resonance imaging: a noninvasive diagnostic procedure employing an MR scanner to obtain detailed sectional images of the internal structure of the body.

Magnesium: The fourth most abundant mineral in the body. It is essential to good health and evident in 300 enzyme reactions. Close to 50% of total body magnesium is found in bone. The other half is found predominantly inside cells of body tissues and organs and 1% is found in the blood.

Maternal inoculations: A first beneficial bacterium a baby receives in its digestive tract comes from the mother during the birthing process.

Metabolic syndrome: A syndrome marked by the presence of usually three or more of a group of factors, such as high blood pressure, abdominal obesity, high triglyceride levels, low HDL levels, and insulin resistance, that are linked to increased risk of cardiovascular disease and type 2 diabetes.

Methamphetamine: A central nervous system stimulant, $C10H15N$, used clinically in the treatment of narcolepsy, hyperkinesia, and for blood pressure maintenance in hypotensive states: also widely used as an illicit drug.

Methicillin: A semi synthetic penicillin antibiotic, $C17H19N2NaO6S$, used principally in the treatment of severe, penicillin-resistant staphylococci infections.

Methionine: An amino acid, $CH3SCH2CH2CH(NH2)COOH$, found in casein, wool, and other proteins or prepared synthetically: used as a supplement to a special diet in the prevention and treatment of certain liver diseases.

Methylation: The process of replacing a hydrogen atom with a methyl group.

Methyltetrahydrafolate gene: One gene that regulates methylation.

Microecology: The ecology of a microhabitat.

Micro flora: Microscopic plants; bacteria are often considered to be microflora.

Microorganisms: Any organism too small to be viewed by the unaided eye, as bacteria, protozoa, and some fungi and algae.

Microvilli: Any of the small, fingerlike projections of the surface of an epithelial cell.

Migraine: An extremely severe paroxysmal headache usually confined to one side of the head and often associated with nausea.

Mineral: Any of a class of substances usually comprising inorganic substances, as quartz or feldspar, of definite chemical composition and usually of definite crystal structure.

Molecule: The smallest physical unit of an element or compound, consisting of one or more like atoms in an element and two or more different atoms in a compound.

Monoglycerides: A glyceride consisting of one fatty acid chain covalently bonded to a glycerol molecule through an ester linkage.

Monomorphism: A one-to-one homomorphism.
Mucopolysaccharides: Any of a class of polysaccharides derived from hexosamine that form mucins when complexed with proteins.

Mucosal Associated Lymphoid Tissue: Mucosal surfaces that come into contact with the outside world have a specialized mucosal immune system.
Mucus: Viscous, slimy mixture of mucins, water, electrolytes, epithelial cells, and leukocytes that is secreted by glands lining the nasal, esophageal, and other body cavities and serves primarily to protect and lubricate surfaces.

Multiple Sclerosis: Chronic degenerative, often episodic disease of the central nervous system marked by patchy destruction of the myelin that surrounds and insulates nerve fibers, usually appearing in young adulthood and manifested by one or more mild to severe neural and muscular impairments, as spastic weakness in one or more limbs, local sensory losses, bladder dysfunction, or visual disturbances.

N

Neurophysiologic condition: consists of anxiolysis, hypnosis, amnesia, and anticonvulsant actions.

Nitrogen: A colorless, odorless, gaseous element that constitutes about four-fifths of the volume of the atmosphere and is present in combined form in animal and vegetable tissues, especially in proteins: used chiefly in the manufacture of ammonia, nitric acid, cyanide, explosives, fertilizer, dyes, as a cooling agent.

Non Steroidal Anti Inflammatory Drugs (NSAID): Drugs with analgesic, antipyretic and, in higher doses, anti-inflammatory effects—they reduce pain, fever and inflammation.

Nutraceuticals: A food or naturally occurring food supplement thought to have a beneficial effect on human health.

O

OCD: Obsessive Compulsive Disorder. An anxiety disorder in which people have thoughts, feelings, ideas, sensations (obsessions), or behaviors that make them feel driven to do something (compulsions).

Obese: Very fat or overweight; corpulent.

Oligomeric Proanthocyandins (OPC's): A class of flavenoids.

Oligosaccharides: A carbohydrate that consists of a

relatively small number of monosaccharides.

Omega 3: An important nutritionally essential unsaturated fatty acid, the body cannot manufacture.

Organism: A form of life composed of mutually interdependent parts that maintain various vital processes.

Orthomolecular: Being or pertaining to the treatment of disease by increasing, decreasing, or otherwise controlling the intake of natural substances, especially vitamins.

Osteoporosis: A disorder in which the bones become increasingly porous, brittle, and subject to fracture, owing to loss of calcium and other mineral components, sometimes resulting in pain, decreased height, and skeletal deformities: common in older persons, primarily postmenopausal women, but also associated with long-term steroid therapy and certain endocrine disorders.

Oxidative: The process or result of oxidizing.

Oxidative stress: A condition of increased oxidant production in animal cells characterized by the release of free radicals and resulting in cellular degeneration.

Oxygen: A colorless, odorless, gaseous element constituting about one-fifth of the volume of the atmosphere and present in a combined state in nature.

P

PANDAS: Pediatric Autoimmune Neuropsychiatric Disorder Associated with Streptococcus.

PMS: A complex of physical and emotional changes, including depression, irritability, appetite changes, bloating and water retention, breast soreness, and changes in muscular coordination, one or more of which may be experienced in the several days before the onset of menstrual flow.

Pancreatic enzymes: Exocrine secretions of the pancreas, mainly for digestion.

Paralysis: A loss or impairment of voluntary movement in a body part, caused by injury or disease of the nerves, brain, or spinal cord.

Pathogen: Any disease-producing agent, especially a virus, bacterium, or other microorganism.

Pediatrics: The branch of medicine concerned with

the development, care, and diseases of babies and children.

Pellagra: A disease caused by a deficiency of niacin in the diet, characterized by skin changes, severe nerve dysfunction, mental symptoms, and diarrhea.

Penicillin: Any of several antibiotics of low toxicity, produced naturally by molds of the genus Penicillium and also semi-synthetically, having a bactericidal action on many susceptible Gram-positive or Gram-negative cocci and bacilli, some also being effective against certain spirochetes.

Pepsin: An enzyme, produced in the stomach, that in the presence of hydrochloric acid splits proteins into proteases and peptones.

Pepsinogen: Crystals, occurring in the gastric glands that during digestion are converted into pepsin.

Peptidase: Any of the class of enzymes that catalyze the hydrolysis of peptides or peptones to amino acids.

Peristalsis: The progressive wave of contraction and relaxation of a tubular muscular system, especially the alimentary canal, by which the contents are forced through the system.

Pernicious Anemia: A severe anemia caused by the diminution or absence of stomach acid secretion, with consequent failure of the gastric mucosa to secrete the intrinsic factor necessary for the absorption of vitamin B12, characterized by a great reduction in the number of red blood cells and an increase in their size.

Pharmaceuticals: A pharmaceutical product or preparation.

Phytonutrients: Any of various bioactive chemical compounds found in plants, as antioxidants, considered to be beneficial to human health.

Pituitary gland: A small, somewhat cherry-shaped double structure attached by a stalk to the base of the brain and constituting the master endocrine gland affecting all hormonal functions in the body. Secreting, LH, FSH, ACTH, TSH, and MSH.

Placenta previa: Pregnancy in which the placenta is implanted in the lower part of the uterus (instead of the upper part); can cause bleeding late in pregnancy; delivery by cesarean section may be necessary.

Pleomorphism: Existence of an organism in two or more distinct forms during the life cycle;

polymorphism.

Polio: An acute viral disease, usually affecting children and young adults, caused by any of three polioviruses, characterized by inflammation of the motor neurons of the brain stem and spinal cord, and resulting in a motor paralysis, followed by muscular atrophy and often permanent deformities.

Polypeptide: A chain of amino acids linked together by peptide bonds and having a molecular weight of up to about 10,000.

Prebiotic: Of or pertaining to chemicals or environmental conditions existing before the development of the first living things.

Preservatives: Something used to preserve, especially a chemical added to foods to inhibit spoilage.

Prilosec: A trademark used for the drug omeprazole, an antacid.

Probiotics: A beneficial bacterium found in the intestinal tract of healthy mammals; often considered to be a plant.

Proline: An alcohol-soluble amino acid,

$C_4H_9NHCOOH$, occurring in high concentration in collagen.

Psoriasis: A common chronic, inflammatory skin disease characterized by scaly patches.

Psychiatry: The practice or science of diagnosing and treating mental disorders.

Pulmonary: Of or pertaining to the lungs.

Pulmonary hypertension: Hypertension in the pulmonary circulation; it may be primary or secondary to pulmonary or cardiac disease.

R

Recommended Daily Allowance of Nutrition (RDA): A system of nutrition recommendations from the Institute of Medicine, part of the US National Academy of Sciences.

Respiratory airway disease: Diseases of the respiratory system.

Rezulin: A trademark used for the drug troglitazone Rheumatism: Any disorder of the extremities or back, characterized by pain and stiffness.

Rheumatoid arthritis: A chronic autoimmune disease characterized by inflammation of the joints, frequently accompanied by marked deformities, and ordinarily associated with manifestations of a general, or systemic, affliction.

Ritalin: A brand of methylphenidate in its hydrochloride form.

Rosacea: A chronic form of acne affecting the nose, forehead, and cheeks, characterized by red pustular lesions.

S

Salmonella: Any of several rod-shaped, facultatively anaerobic bacteria of the genus Salmonella, as S. typhosa, that may enter the digestive tract of humans and other mammals in contaminated food and cause abdominal pains and violent diarrhea.

Scurvy: Disease marked by swollen and bleeding gums, livid spots on the skin, prostration, etc., due to a diet lacking in vitamin C.

Serotonin: A neurotransmitter, derived from tryptophan that is involved in sleep, depression, memory, and other neurological processes.

Shigella: Any of several rod-shaped aerobic bacteria of the genus Shigella, certain species of which are pathogenic for humans and other warm-blooded animals.

Sinus: One of the hollow cavities in the skull connecting with the nasal cavities.

Small Intestines: The narrow, longer part of the intestines, comprising the duodenum, jejunum, and ileum, that serves to digest and absorb nutrients.

Staph: Any of several spherical bacteria of the genus Staphylococcus, occurring in pairs, tetrads, and irregular clusters, certain species of which, as S. aureus, can be pathogenic for humans.

Steroid: Any of a large group of fat-soluble organic compounds, as the sterols, bile acids, and sex hormones, most of which have specific physiological action.

Stomach: A saclike enlargement of the alimentary canal, as in humans and certain animals, forming an organ for storing, diluting, and digesting food.

Streptococcus: Any of several spherical or oval bacteria of the genus Streptococcus, occurring in pairs or chains, certain species of which are pathogenic for humans, causing scarlet fever, tonsillitis, etc.

Stroke: A blockage or hemorrhage of a blood vessel leading to the brain, causing inadequate oxygen supply and, depending on the extent and location of the abnormality, such symptoms as weakness, paralysis of parts of the body, speech difficulties, and, if severe, loss of consciousness or death.

Sugar: A sweet, crystalline substance, $C_{12}H_{22}O_{11}$, obtained chiefly from the juice of the sugarcane and the sugar beet, and present in sorghum, maple sap, etc.: used extensively as an ingredient and flavoring of certain foods and as a fermenting agent in the manufacture of certain alcoholic beverages; sucrose.

Supplementation: The act or process of supplementing.

Synovial sac: A thin tissue that lines the joint.

Synthesizing: To form (a material or abstract entity) by combining parts or elements.

Systemic enzymes: Enzymes used systemically in the body.

T

Tagamet: A brand of cimetidine, an antacid.

Tetracycline: An antibiotic, $C_{22}H_{24}H_2O_8$, derived from chlortetracycline, used in medicine to treat a broad variety of infections.

Theta Waves: Brain waves observed during sleep or during quiet contemplation or daydreaming.

Thimerosal: A cream-colored, crystalline, water-soluble powder, $C_9H_9HgNaO_2S$, used chiefly as an antiseptic.

Thrush: An infection of the mouth caused by Candida fungus, also known as yeast.

Thyroid stimulating hormone (TSH): A glycoprotein hormone secreted by the anterior portion of the pituitary gland that stimulates and regulates the activity of the thyroid gland.

Thyrotoxicosis: A disease characterized by an enlarged thyroid, a rapid pulse, and increased basal metabolism due to excessive thyroid secretion; exophthalmic goiter.

Toxins: A poisonous substance, especially a protein, that is produced by living cells or organisms and is capable of causing disease when introduced into the body tissues but is often also capable of inducing neutralizing antibodies or antitoxins.

U

Upper Respiratory Infection: Infection of the upper respiratory tract.

Urinary Tract Infections: An infection that can happen anywhere along the urinary tract.

Urticaria: A transient condition of the skin usually caused by an allergic reaction, characterized by pale or reddened irregular, elevated patches and severe itching; hives.

V

Vaccination: The act or practice of vaccinating; inoculation with vaccine.

Vaginitis: Inflammation of the vagina.

Valine: An essential amino acid, $(CH_3)_2CHCH(NH_2)COOH$, white, crystalline, and water-soluble, present in most plant and animal proteins, required for growth.

Ventricular septal defect: A common congenital heart defect; an abnormal opening in the septum dividing the ventricles allows blood to pass directly from the left to the right ventricle; large openings may cause congestive heart failure.

Vibrio cholerae: A bacterium that causes Asiatic cholera in humans; Koch's bacillus.

Villi: One of the minute, wormlike processes on certain membranes, especially on the mucous membrane of the small intestine, where they serve in absorbing nutriment.

Virus: An ultramicroscopic (20 to 300 nm in diameter), metabolically inert, infectious agent that replicates only within the cells of living hosts, mainly bacteria, plants, and animals: composed of an RNA or DNA core, a protein coat, and, in more complex types, a surrounding envelope.

Vitamin: Any of a group of organic substances essential in small quantities to normal metabolism, found in minute amounts in natural foodstuffs or sometimes produced synthetically: deficiencies of vitamins produce specific disorders.

Vitiligo: A skin disorder characterized by smooth, white patches on various parts of the body, caused by the loss of the natural pigment.

W

Water-soluble: Capable of dissolving in water.

Y

Yeast infection: A disease characterized by itching and irritation of the vagina, vulva, or other mucous membranes, with a yeasty-smelling discharge.

INDEX

NOTES